Stepping Out
of the Boat

(a year of miracles)

By James M. Thayer

For my mom,

Your faith in Jesus to heal me, so many years ago,
is framed and hung in the heavens as the seed
that produced so much of His glory in my life.

Seek First Productions, LLC - established 2012

Edited by Dona J. Dyer

ISBN: 9798987786703

Library of Congress Control Number: 2023902595

Contents

FOREWORD

I remember the day in 2012; I was standing in a church meeting in Adelaide, Australia listening to a man tell stories of mind-blowing healing miracles. He told story after story of the impossible being interrupted by the supernatural. My nerves were racing as I walked to the front to be prayed for. When the man walked up to me, it was like he was looking directly into my soul with eyes of fire. He asked me, "What can I do for you, sir?" I sheepishly replied, "To be honest, I want to believe everything you are saying, but I don't." I was afraid of what he would say to me, but then he responded very gently, "Well, the good news is you are still here; everyone else would have left by now." He then prayed for me, and nothing happened. I returned to my seat as the man continued praying for everyone at the meeting.

When he was done, my mother-in-law looked at me and said, "You should go up again." Being naturally a little prideful, I usually would not have, but this time was different; I was desperate for something more to my Christianity than I had been living. So there I found myself back at the front of the church.

As the man walked up to me again, he said with a smirk, "So what can I do for you *now*?" I replied, "Honestly, my mother-in-law made me come." He laughed and then pulled a handkerchief out of his pocket and gently whipped me in my stomach with it - and that was when everything changed.

The moment I felt that handkerchief brush across my torso, the power of God came upon me in a way it never had before, and the heavy weight of His glory began to push me down to the ground. I tried to resist, but I eventually gave in. With my face pressed against the dusty floor, I wept for the next twenty minutes as skepticism and unbelief were being torn out of my spirit.

From that moment on, I was never the same; my life of living in the miraculous began. I don't have time here to tell you all the wild, mind-baffling miracles I have seen since that day. However, I do want to say this. I opened this foreword with that story because, as I read the pages of this book, I felt a rush of the presence of God; I felt the Holy Spirit stirring in me again for yet greater things. I felt the

Holy Spirit begin to challenge me not to allow life and busyness to position me in a place of complacency. I felt the Holy Spirit remind me not to live on yesterday's testimonies but to live intentionally to see miracles daily.

This book is for the skeptics and unbelievers, so don't put it down if that's you. This book is for those with questions; this book is for those who are hungry to live a life of miracles. This book is for those with plenty of testimonies from the past but not so many from the present. So if that's you, allow the Spirit of God to breathe His breath of life on the embers in your soul so that you would rise again and burn with a passion for the miraculous.

I have been privileged to watch James' journey from genuine questions to real action. His passion, dedication, and tenacity to destroy the works of the devil are inspiring, challenging, and contagious. If the devil were in the details, James would cast him out to ensure he could keep the details because his desire for a true story far outweighs his desire for a good story. Let me tell you, the stories you will read in this book are true. The stories you will read in this book are just the beginning.

His humility and vulnerability in his writing should be noted, as they are two of the best keys to living a life of miracles. My prayer as you read this book is not just that you would be entertained, because you will be, but that God, by His Spirit, would do in you what he did in me and what he has done in James.

As you read this book, I pray that you will never be the same, and that you will be stirred to believe that a supernatural God will do supernatural things around you and through you. I pray you will be filled with the gift of faith to believe that you would lay hands on the sick and they would recover, that you would drive out demons and they would leave, and that you would never forget this; there is only one way to walk on water, and that is to step out of the boat. God does miracles through those who believe. God has the power; we are the vessel, we get the privilege, and God gets the glory. Amen.

- Pastor Joel Ramsey, Citipointe Nashville

Introduction

It is Sunday, December 12th, 2021, and I am sitting in church a few rows back from the front. Everyone is singing worship songs to God, but I'm praying. It is a prayer I've sent heavenward countless times over the past three months since I decided to step out of the boat and ask for miracles. I ask God again to "please let me lay hands on the sick and see them healed."

There is an interlude in worship where a pastor steps on stage and asks anyone in the audience that needs prayer to raise their hand. A man directly in front of me, whom I'd later come to know as Kevin, raises his hand slightly. As I had done the past three months many times before, I stepped forward, put my hand on Kevin's shoulder, and began to pray.

I did not know what I was praying for (something that continues to bother me to this day when the church decides to generically pray for people), but on this morning it did not matter. Why? Because the Holy Spirit knew what I needed to pray for, and for the first time since I began to step out of the boat, He wasn't going to let me sink. My thumb began to rub back and forth slightly on Kevin's shoulder, and I did not know why. I remember thinking, "That's really strange and probably inappropriate," but my thumb kept doing it anyway.

I prayed simply, "Body be healed in the name of Jesus!" Then, suddenly, I felt movement beneath my hand. Muscles began to shift inside the shoulder. I became quite worried - I thought I might have injured him. I distinctly remember thinking, "This guy must have some serious medical issues if I just broke his shoulder by putting my hand on it."

There came a loud cracking noise; it sounded like bone breaking. Kevin began to weep, and then he started to laugh. I did not know what was going on; I was not familiar with the sights and sounds of a miracle at this time. Thankfully, Kevin turned around and cleared things up for me. He said, "Right where you placed your hand, I've had a shoulder injury for months. I've been unable to lift my arm above my chest since then, but God just healed me!" My mind began to race, and I felt the weight of the Holy Spirit. At last, I had seen what I knew was possible, but up until that point felt it was just out of reach. For months I had been praying for people, but I never saw anyone instantly healed like this. I began to cry.

"Crying" doesn't fully encapsulate what my spirit was doing. It was like I had stored up all of my feelings in a jar, and then someone with gentle hands came along to pour them out. My heart was naked before God; I could only worship in gratitude. If you've ever had a moment where you were genuinely thankful and knew you could never repay someone for something they had done for you, you might know the feeling I'm talking about. I ran out of the church, found a place out back where I could be alone, and let the Holy Spirit direct my worship there.

Since that day, I've seen dozens of miracles. I've seen God burn terminal illnesses out, dissolve kidney stones, realign vertebrae, and drive demons out of people - instantly freeing them of spiritual sickness. I've seen Him save marriages on the brink of collapse, stop a miscarriage, and open the womb of the infertile. Since that day, I've had scales fall from my eyes, revealing the horrors of the spiritual war raging around us. And I have learned the modern church is ill-prepared to deal with the American mission field.

I spent twenty years of my Christian walk devouring every bit of theology, scripture, and philosophy I could get my hands on. Naturally prone to debate, I spent untold days arguing for the existence of God and "tearing down arguments" against Him as Paul did in 2 Corinthians 10:5. I like to think I planted seeds and watered some that others had already instilled, but I do not believe I ever directly led anyone to Jesus during that time.

For twenty years, I lived the Christian life in my own strength and in ignorance of the Holy Spirit's work. I did not talk to Him, I did not acknowledge what He desired to do in my world or the lives of others, and I dragged Him into my sin - grieving Him in the process.

During this time, I lived in incredible frustration. I would read the promises of Christ and see how the Church lived in the book of Acts - then I'd compare it to my own life. My wife, Aly, had similar issues. The pandemic of 2020 only compounded our despair as we were kept from corporate worship - truly the only place I ever heard clearly and specifically from God.

We came out of the pandemic asking ourselves, "Is this it? Is this all Christianity is? We go to church on Sunday, read our bibles, pray a little throughout the week, and just die one day?" In hindsight, these questions were coming to the surface because the Holy Spirit was drawing us into the "abundant life" Jesus had preached in John 10:10. At the time though, we did not understand why both of us, without even discussing it with one another, desired to break from nominal Christianity.

Things came to a head on September 9th, 2021 (roughly three months before Kevin's shoulder was miraculously healed). I asked Aly what she wanted to do for her birthday, and to my surprise, she wanted to see a traveling evangelist named Shane Winnings who was stopping by Nashville to preach to a small crowd. We could never have imagined what that night would do to our faith. Jesus said a seed must die before it can become fruitful. I truly believe something in me died that night, and by the grace of God I've been living an abundant life ever since.

Everything I thought was extraordinary about myself I've since given up, and in exchange I've found a new Friend, the Holy Spirit, who has done things I never in a thousand lifetimes could have imagined He would do.

I want to share with you what exactly happened to me because I know it can happen to you too. If we follow Jesus, the same Spirit that raised Christ from the dead lives inside us (Romans 6:10). The real question is, do we believe it? Are we willing to put to death the restrictive doctrines of man that have made our churches so impotent to tear down the works of darkness? Are we willing to allow our faith to embarrass us if it means we get to attempt to do the will of the Father? Do we believe Christ enough to step out of the boat like Peter? I'm here to tell you that God is calling us into an abundant life of righteousness, deep intimacy with our Creator, and a walk filled with miracles, signs, and wonders - which are becoming increasingly necessary to reach a dark world for Jesus. The question is, "Will we answer that call?"

Chapter 1
The First Miracle

I want to tell you about the first miracle I ever experienced to give you insight into how numb a person can become to the Holy Spirit's desires. When I was ten years old I was nihilistic and depressed. My wife likes to say this would be laughable for most ten-year-olds unless you knew me personally and my proclivity to think deeply about things. One day, my pediatrician diagnosed me with clinical depression and told my mom I should see a therapist. Mom offered that option, but likewise said she'd like to take me to church if I was willing. I, thank the Lord, said "Yes."

I did not agree with what the Christians in the church believed at first, but I kept on attending because I liked the people and activities. After roughly nine months my mom approached me one day to say a man was planting a church down the street from us who "had the gift of prophecy." This was incredibly intriguing to me, so I decided to go with her and my brother to a small evening service. I do not remember what the man preached, all I remember is at the end he called people forward for prayer.

You must understand how pivotal of a moment it is for someone to walk down to the altar of a church. Those few paces can save their life, save their soul, heal their body, or deliver them from a past of pain. Altar calls are quickly becoming the time I most pine for. Give me lines, thousands deep, of people wanting prayer, and I'll be a happy camper. I'm not even sure I'd require much food if I were put in that situation. I like to believe I'd be able to share in the heavenly food Jesus spoke about in John 4:32.

For me, that short journey to the front meant *everything*. The preacher put his hand on my forehead, and I did something not quite out of my will, but rather something I'd will to happen forever if I had much choice in the matter. I *fell* backward. This must have been a regular occurrence because there were people there ready for it, and they gently laid me on the floor.

Immediately a rush of peace came over me. I felt an indescribable love from God. It was as if He was

immersing me in it - immersing me in *Himself.*
Then I began to see visions - only one of which the
meaning has been made clear to me in the past
couple of years. The man praying over me began to
tell me strange things about my future life. If the
whole thing wasn't tape-recorded, I would not have
been able to remember them. Fortunately, my mom
was wise enough to get the tape, write everything
down, and discuss it with me.

The man told me I would be an evangelist. He said I
was filled with the Holy Spirit in the womb, like
John the Baptist.

I find it interesting that in the past couple of years I
have felt an affinity for John in scripture. His call to
repentance was so simple. People didn't go out to
him in the wilderness to see a laser light show; they
came because they wanted to know God. John had a
revelation to share with them, and he would baptize
them as a symbol of repentance - of turning from
their old ways towards the ways of God. The man
ate locusts, wore camel hair, and was probably
nothing handsome to look at. But the Spirit of God
was inside of him from his very birth, and it is the
Holy Spirit who draws people to the Father. Don't

miss this. People did not go to John because he had anything to offer them aside from an authentic encounter with their Creator. Our churches today could stand to learn something from him.

The prophecy I received was great, even though it didn't mean anything to me at the time. The visions were great, even though they too were just as mysterious. But for a ten-year-old who was skipping classes, had alienated all of his peers, and was wondering if life had any meaning or purpose at all - it was what God took *away* that made such a difference. He instantly and miraculously took my depression away. I did not know at the time that I would see this miracle happen in person after person I pray for today.

Looking back, what is shocking, is how I failed to realize it wasn't the man praying for me who was special - it was the God *inside* of him. We read in scripture time and time again how God makes His home in those who follow Jesus. Why then did it take me so long to put two and two together? If the God of the universe was in that man, and through him I received revelation along with freedom from sickness in my soul, why did I never stop to ask God in the twenty subsequent years I followed Him to start doing such things through me?

I'm sure Satan had some direct hand in the matter - stealing the word and all of that - but I also believe I fell victim to false doctrines of my own making.

Chapter 2
"He's prayed for me many times, and I've never been healed."

September 9th, 2021, was not only my wife's birthday but also a day of spiritual *re*birthing for us, that occurred roughly 20 years after I was freed from depression. As I previously mentioned, Shane Winnings was a traveling evangelist who came to Nashville that night to preach and pray for people. I was going because I wanted to please my wife, but if I knew then what I know now I would have traded anything to be there.

Shane and one of his companions set up on a concrete platform in an unassuming park. People began to file in, and the crowd was much smaller than I anticipated - I'd say no more than 30-40 people came. He preached a sermon about how God had not saved us *just* so we could go to heaven, but that He had a real adventure for us to endeavor in the here and now too. After speaking, Shane gave a simple call for anyone needing prayer to line up. A line formed that comprised at least half of the total number there - including my mother who had a terminal lung illness.

Try to imagine my wife and I on this night. We had both, separately but now together, been asking God to show us there was more to the Christian faith than we had been experiencing. This soft-spoken ex-military man was standing at the head of a line of sick people and his plan was simple - pray for them. He tells the people in the queue not to go into too much detail about their illness but to give him the basics.

This is the most effective way I have ever seen anybody evangelize the lost. I previously cited 2 Corinthians, where Paul talks about taking arguments against God captive. Sometime after this night, I opened up 1 Corinthians 2, and this verse burned itself in my brain: "My message and my preaching were not with wise and persuasive words, but with a demonstration of the Spirit's power, so that your faith might not rest on human wisdom, but on God's power."

"He's prayed for me many times, and I've never been healed."

A demonstration of God's power! How exciting and how bold. You will find a theme constantly repeated in the New Testament if you open your eyes to it: the kingdom of God is not about talk, but about power (1 Corinthians 4:20). Here was a man willing to make himself look foolish if it meant the gospel could be spread. Anyone who prays for the sick will tell you that not everyone is healed, so to ask God to heal a person "now" is a big step of faith which can leave you looking silly if the person is not remedied (you step out of the boat, you sink fast!) Shane wasn't worried about that - he loved these people, and out of that love he would be willing to play the part of the fool if it meant they might encounter God. Perfect love casts out fear, and that is the secret to overcoming it.

One after the other, people came up for prayer, and about 70% of them were miraculously and instantly healed. Aly and I saw a wheel-chair bound girl get up and walk, and by the end of the night she was dancing. Later we'd see medical confirmation God healed her of the disease that caused her previous affliction. Demons were coming out of people. A woman fell straight to the ground, and her legs shook violently. Shane calmly commanded the evil spirit to come out of the woman, and so it did. She cried tears of joy. It eventually became my mom's turn to receive prayer, and unfortunately she was not instantly healed. I will discuss what our response should be when someone is not healed in a later chapter.

After all of this was over, I felt like I needed to talk to Shane, so I waited until I could grab his attention and began, "I love seeing what you do. When I became a Christian, somebody prophesied that I would be an evangelist like you, but I haven't seen anything like this in my life. I keep asking God for a ministry, but I don't know what it looks like. He told me to build a house, so I think it has something to do with that. Also, the gift of healing you have is amazing. I've prayed for many people and I've never seen any of them healed..."

At this point, my mom cut in and threw me under the bus in a kind-hearted joking manner. "Oh yes, I know he doesn't have that gift - he's prayed for me many times and I've not been healed."

I thought this might be the end of the conversation, but Shane asked if he could pray for me, and I certainly was not going to turn him down after what I'd just witnessed. He prayed along these lines: "God, I pray for James. That you would inconvenience him for the gospel. I pray he finds himself preaching the gospel in grocery stores and preaching the gospel to the detriment of his schedule. I also pray for these hands - that he would lay them on the sick, and the sick would recover."

I know you're probably wondering if I felt anything as he prayed this prayer, and I'll tell you right now that expecting to "feel" something is walking by sight. As he walked on the water, the waves distracted Peter, and he began to sink. We must stop walking by sight and trust that Jesus isn't a liar. If He says something, it is true. For example, many of us often wonder if God is with us. We base the belief that He may not be on the fact that we can't feel His presence at times, but this is walking by sight rather than faith. Belief is worth infinitely more than sensory input.

I did not feel anything I can recall, but I thanked the man and headed back to the car with my family. On the way though, my mind began to turn. I resolved that I would at least *try* to pray for the sick and try to step out of the boat. Shane did arm me with one piece of knowledge that I'd come back to time and time again to encourage myself. He said he prayed for over five-hundred people before seeing a miracle. Later I'd find out a man who famously prays for the sick named Todd White prayed for roughly nine-hundred people before *he* ever saw a miracle.

God is so good. He does not treat us as we deserve. I wouldn't pray for nearly that number of people before I'd start seeing fruit. I was determined to pray for anyone I could lay my hands on. Up until this point I thought I was a bold man, but I'd soon find out how little courage I truly possessed.

Chapter 3
"Aly, please tell me to go pray for her."

Several weeks into my journey of praying for the sick, I found myself in a Connecticut hotel lobby enjoying a continental breakfast with strangers around who were doing the same. Suddenly, out of the low hum of people eating, came a groan. An older woman, clearly in pain, was shuffling through the line, putting a plate of food together. She continued to groan with each movement she made. It was at that moment I realized I was in a terrible predicament. I had resolved to pray for the sick, and a few tables over was a woman who was clearly ill. Yet, she didn't know me at all, and the room was full of strangers going about their business. This was a place of dignified digestion and certainly not a place to pray for a sick person. *Also*, I was done eating, and I *really* should have been off to my next engagement.

When you're in public and feel compelled to pray

for the sick, thoughts such as these will flood your mind. You will come up with any excuse possible to get out of walking up to a stranger and asking if you can pray for them - especially when you aren't seeing anyone healed!

I remember a time not too long ago when I was filming a Christian concert, and as such I was privy to the artists backstage. I noticed something different about the young woman who happened to be the opening act - she walked with a cane. It was clearly something she had been used to doing for some time as she almost integrated it into her personality and dress. Those thoughts came flooding in, "You're on the job; this would be awkward; she's a Christian, so someone has probably already prayed for her; she's a celebrity, and people are taking photos with her - this isn't the right time or place."

I'm ashamed to say I did not pray for the musician. Whether my conviction was too weak, or Satan overcame me, or even if it seriously was the wrong time, I do not know. What I do know is I want those occurrences to become less and less in my life until they are eradicated. So let me pose a question to you. If you had a superpower where you could instantly heal anyone by simply touching them and saying a few words, how much would you have to hate a person not to heal them? This question is similar to the one famous magician Penn Jillette once posed to his online audience: If you genuinely believed someone was going to hell unless they heard the gospel, how much would you have to hate that person not to share the gospel with them? Keep in mind Penn was a militant atheist when he said this.

How is the heart of an atheist more broken for the lost of our world than the heart of a Christian? The truth is, you have the superpower to heal the sick inside you - His name is Holy Spirit. I'll get into the theology behind this in a later chapter, but for now you must understand what stepping onto the water might mean for someone else. The risk is only your reputation, but the reward could be a person's life changed forever. More so, it could be a person's *soul* being checked out of hell and into heaven. Eternity is in the balance when we're deciding to love someone as Christ loves them - being willing to play the part of the fool if it helps another person.

I'm not ashamed to admit it because I think it's profoundly funny, but I sat in that hotel lobby in Connecticut for a solid 5 minutes staring out of the window. From the outside, I looked like a statue, but on the inside a war was raging between God's call on my life and my pride. My solution, therefore, was to use my pride against itself. So I opened my phone and texted my wife, "There is a woman I need to pray for. Please tell me to go pray for her." I knew I could easily punk out, walk away, and no one else would have to know about it. Yet I'm a prideful man who doesn't want to be seen as a coward in front of my wife. I knew if I told her, I'd be held accountable to her.

Before Aly could text me back, a little blonde girl walked over to me. She was roughly my daughter Josephine's age at this time – one and a half years old. She looked up at me and smiled broadly. I then panned my head to the left and saw the woman in pain staring at her. We locked eyes and I took my shot, "She's adorable; how old is she?"

The woman's husband had left the table momentarily to grab more food. The little girl happened to be her granddaughter, and after talking about my daughters (Ella and Josie, as we like to call Josephine) for a moment I was invited to sit at her table. The husband returned and eventually I was able to ask about her injuries.

It turns out this woman used to be a drug addict. She contracted MRSA, a violent bacterial infection resistant to antibiotics, from snorting tainted cocaine a long time ago. The infection spread rapidly throughout her system. To save her life, they had to do invasive surgery, leaving her with wounds that never fully healed. I asked her if she minded if I prayed for her to be healed, which she was grateful for. I put my hand on her shoulder, lifted her up to God, and commanded her body to be healed in the name of Jesus.

I then asked if she could tell if there was any change, and she told me that she felt "tingly." In a later chapter I'll get into practical aspects of praying for the sick, but one thing you should know is that the Holy Spirit often makes people feel tingly or warm when He is healing them. In this case, though, tingly was all the woman experienced at that time - there was no instantaneous healing.

Looking back, I probably should have prayed a second time for her.

I was disappointed but also proud of myself for stepping out of the boat. At that moment I thought I heard from God, "Love her," so that's what I did. I asked her about her life story and even tried to practically help her with a business endeavor she was undertaking. I encouraged her in the faith - reminding her of God's great love for her and the gospel message.

And God taught me a lesson in humility. I was not as bold as I thought I was. Deep down, I have a good deal of what the bible calls "fear of man." In other words, I don't want to look foolish and sometimes fear what *people* might think about me more than fearing what *God* might think about me. This is something I've had to mortify - and continue to put to death to this day.

You'll be relieved to know that I have never had anyone be angry with me after praying for them, and I've only been turned down twice after offering to pray for someone in public. Whether or not they are healed, those who accept prayer always feel loved.

One time my wife and I were swinging through a BBQ place when we sat down next to a much older couple. Aly remarked, "That poor man, he can barely walk," as she witnessed the husband shuffle to the bathroom. I resolved to strike up a conversation with the wife of the couple in an effort to find a way to pray for her husband. It turned out the woman herself had an issue with one of her organs that caused her great embarrassment. I asked her if I could pray for her, and she immediately broke down crying. She said that was the first time anyone had ever asked to pray for her to be healed. The woman felt loved. Understand that sometimes God has us pray for people to be healed and we might be disappointed when they aren't, but a seed has been planted.

I was once on a flight coming back from Washington D.C. where I had just finished filming a concert. The woman I sat next to happened to be a politician coming back from an LGBTQ conference. She was in a lesbian relationship, considered herself a "spiritualist," and said one of the most offensive things I believe anyone has ever said to me in public. Yet I knew God loved her - she was His daughter! So I endeavored to share the gospel with her and finally got my chance about twenty minutes before we landed.

She was stunned by it. She confided in me that no one had ever shared such a thing with her before. This woman must have been in her fifties, so to hear *that* shocked me. She thanked me for sharing the gospel with her on her way off the plane, multiple times.

You may be the first person to ever pray for someone or preach the gospel to someone, and it might change their entire outlook on both God and the Church.

Will we do it though? Will we step out, at significant risk to our reputation, and boldly proclaim the good news while praying for the sick? If you don't feel like that's something you could ever do, fear not because you're in great company. In the next chapter, I want to illuminate what God can do with fearful and even unbelieving people - He can turn the world upside down with them.

Chapter 4
A Bunch of Unbelievers

I cannot take credit for drawing out the implications of this passage I want to discuss. I wholeheartedly admit I've borrowed this revelation from Reinhard Bonnke, an evangelist who brought over 75 million people to Christ in the last century. Alas, this passage of scripture has made the most sense to me concerning how some people can boldly proclaim the gospel or pray for the sick, while others cannot.

In Mark chapter 16 we find Jesus has been resurrected from the dead. He shows up to Mary Magdalene, who then runs to tell the disciples she's seen the risen Savior. Verse eleven records, "When they heard that Jesus was alive and that she had seen him, they did not believe it."

They did not believe!

After this, Jesus shows up to two disciples while

walking on a road. These two disciples then run to tell the other disciples, and verse thirteen records, "These returned and reported it to the rest; but they did not believe them either."

So again, these men of supposed great faith who walked with Jesus in the flesh were considered unbelievers!

Finally, Jesus appears to His eleven remaining (Judas was dead at this point) apostles, and verse fourteen tells us: "He rebuked them for their lack of faith and their stubborn refusal to believe those who had seen Him after He had risen."

Do you see this pattern? Three times the gospel of Mark records the disciples as unbelieving in chapter 16 - the very thing Jesus rebuked them for in Matthew 17 regarding their inability to heal a young demon-possessed boy. What is astounding is what Jesus says next to them.

"Go into all the world and preach the gospel to all creation," Jesus tells them in verse fifteen. We can then skip down to verse twenty, and we find the disciples indeed went into the world, made disciples, and miraculous signs followed their ministry. What changed? How did a bunch of unbelievers turn into mighty men of God who could heal the sick, drive out demons, preach despite horrid persecution, and even raise the dead? The secret is found in what had to occur between the time Jesus told them to go out and the time they actually went out. We know, chronologically, Acts 2 happened - Pentecost.

Chapter 5
How Can a Mere Man Heal?

My wife and I had just finished ministering to a friend going through a rough patch. God had given this man a vision of Jesus as he lay on our couch, and Jesus had given him instruction on how to overcome addictions plaguing his life. This was exciting enough, but I felt like God wanted to do something else in his life to bless him. He had been complaining about a shoulder injury earlier in the day so I offered to pray for his healing, which he accepted.

I placed my hand on his shoulder, and my wife put hers on his back. I then commanded the shoulder to be completely healed in the name of Jesus. Sure enough, he began to feel tingly. I rebuked the pain, which melted away, starting from his shoulder and ending at the base of his spine. Something in his back released, and for the first time in years the man could feel his lower left back while all the pain simultaneously left his shoulder.

This wasn't the first miracle he had experienced in our living room. He'd come from a cessationist background - which means he did not believe God still does miracles through His Church. It is hard to deny God does miracles though, when He does them in your own life. Yet, my friend was still holding onto a spirit of religion.

"I hope ya'll don't believe you heal people," he exclaimed. I put my hand on his shoulder again and told him, "Do you think anyone can pop their hand on a person and command them to be healed and they will be healed? Do you think a man can heal another man? Of course not. The Holy Spirit has healed you. I can't heal alone, but God, through me, can heal anyone." This satisfied his desire to retain some of that doctrine I'm believing one day the Church will be free of.

So what exactly happened to the disciples at Pentecost? Many believe this is when they first received the Holy Spirit, but that isn't scriptural. In John 20:22, before Pentecost, we find Jesus breathed on His disciples, and that's when they received the Holy Spirit. On the contrary, Acts 1:8 tells us the Holy Spirit came upon the disciples at Pentecost to give them "power."

When a Christian makes Jesus their Lord, the Holy
Spirit takes residence inside them. Ephesians 1 tells
us the Holy Spirit is the downpayment on our eternal inheritance. Believing and having the Spirit live
inside us is not the same as being baptized in the
Holy Spirit, though. Many people want to argue
there is no such thing as the baptism of the Holy
Spirit, but again this doctrine is not found in scripture - to the contrary, I can show you two places
where followers of Jesus had yet to be baptized in
the Spirit.

The first is found in Acts 8. Philip, a great evangelist in the early church, is converting droves of people in Samaria through his preaching, healing, and
deliverance. In response to this good news, the
apostles put a plan into action:

"When the apostles in Jerusalem heard that Samaria
had accepted the word of God, they sent Peter and
John to Samaria. When they arrived, they prayed
for the new believers there that they might receive
the Holy Spirit, **because the Holy Spirit had not
yet come on any of them; they had simply been**

baptized in the name of the Lord Jesus. Then Peter and John placed their hands on them, and they received the Holy Spirit."

The second instance is found in Acts 19 when Paul is ministering in Ephesus:

"There he found some disciples and asked them, **"Did you receive the Holy Spirit when you believed?"** They answered, "No, we have not even heard that there is a Holy Spirit."** So Paul asked, "Then what baptism did you receive?" "John's baptism," they replied. Paul said, "John's baptism was a baptism of repentance. He told the people to believe in the one coming after him, that is, in Jesus." On hearing this, they were baptized in the name of the Lord Jesus. When Paul placed his hands on them, the Holy Spirit came on them, and they spoke in tongues and prophesied. There were about twelve men in all."

Notice that in both cases there are groups of believers, Christ followers, who have not been baptized in the Holy Spirit. Remember what John the Baptist said about Jesus in Matthew 3?

"I baptize you with water for repentance. But after me comes one who is more powerful than I, whose sandals I am not worthy to carry. He will baptize you with the Holy Spirit and fire."

Thus, there are *two* baptisms found in scripture. The first is John's baptism - a baptism in water and of repentance. The symbolism of this baptism is excellent, and Christians are urged to do it, but this is not the same as the baptism Jesus brought - one in the Holy Spirit and with fire.

A good friend of mine has a wife who grew up in a church that did not believe in this second baptism. She said the people closest to her who talked about the Holy Spirit were kind of "weird" about it. I should take a moment to note that when the Holy Spirit came upon the disciples at Pentecost, they too were kind of weird about it. So much so, those observing them claimed the men must be drunk (Acts 2:15)! What the Holy Spirit does *can* seem strange to our eyes, but He is a perfect gentleman. He does not force Himself upon anyone. He loves to be invited, and He is grieved when He is ignored.

Try to put yourself in the shoes of this woman. She

wasn't much different from my wife and I. She sus-
pected there was more to Christianity than she had
been told, yet she was uncomfortable with how others close to her spoke about the Holy Spirit.

For example, one night after dinner (she specifically
asked to come over so I might explain the Holy
Spirit to her), she told my wife and I a story about a
man she knew who claimed to have a tremendous
spiritual experience in his bedroom. After this experience, he became "quite extreme" - wanting to pray
for people's healing in public, for example. Yet, his
character did not align with that of a God-fearing
man. I asked her if the extreme man's wife was
afraid of him. She responded, yes she was, and that
one time they were driving down the highway and
the man jumped out of the car because a voice had
told him to kill himself.

I told her in no sugar-coated terms that I believed
this man *did* have a great spiritual experience, but
that it was not with the Holy Spirit - but rather a
demon coming disguised as an angel of light. Holy
Spirit does not make people fear; He certainly
doesn't tell people to kill themselves. I told her *that*
story had Satan written all over it. Scripturally we

are given several qualities concerning the Holy Spirit. For one, He produces particular *fruit* in the believer's life - things like love, patience, self-control, etc. These "fruits" are the character traits of God. Likewise, we are told Holy Spirit imparts *gifts* to the believer. These gifts include things like faith to perform miracles, prophecy, or speaking in tongues. Be wary of the person who claims to possess the *gifts*, but their life is devoid of the *fruit*. Satan can perform false miracles, but he can't produce anything honorable.

So I spent a good hour telling my friend's wife about the Holy Spirit - citing scripture along the way. She loved what I was saying and knew about the miracles I had been claiming, so eventually she brought up her terrible anxiety. She had been suffering from panic attacks along with depression. I'm at a point in my life where I believe there is a time to shut up, quit arguing about God, and let Him speak for Himself. Remember, the kingdom of God is not about talk but about power.

I asked her if my wife and I could pray for God to remove her anxiety, and she bravely agreed. We got down on the floor of our living room, and I com-

manded the evil spirit to leave her. It did! She felt
the thing lift off her, and in its place came the peace
of the Holy Spirit. Remember, God has not given
you a spirit of fear - He has given you the Holy
Spirit, and from Him we receive power, love, and a
sound mind (2 Timothy 1:7).

Then something else miraculous happened - the
Holy Spirit gave my wife a word of knowledge. Now
a word of knowledge is part of the prophetic gifting.
It is when God tells you something about someone
else, or a specific situation, you could not have
known by natural means. God told my wife that the
woman we were praying for had terrible pain in her
shoulders and back. Stepping out of the boat, my
wife asked if this was true, and of course the woman
said "yes."

Aly then began to pray for the woman's back to be
healed, and guess what? It was healed. At that
point, I asked the woman if she'd like to receive the
Holy Spirit herself. She had a taste of His goodness
and desired much more. I then laid my hand on her,
lifted her up to God, and prayed for her to receive
the Holy Spirit. The Spirit of God then came upon
her in such love and peace that she wanted to lie

down. Do you remember me telling you what happened to me when the man with the gift of prophecy prayed over me? Feeling so much peace you want to lie down is not uncommon when a person falls under the weight of the Holy Spirit.

From that day on, she and her husband were lit on fire for the Lord. Weeks later, I received a follow-up that this woman was now talking and walking with the Holy Spirit - that she was meeting the same hostility from her parents that she once had towards others who spoke about the miraculous. Yet, because she now was baptized in the Spirit, she had the boldness to preach the good news of her deliverance despite it.

Holy Spirit took a group of unbelievers, as described in Mark 16, and turned them into a group of people that flipped this world on its head. He took an anxiety-ridden doubting young woman and not only healed her but put boldness in her too. Do you remember me telling you about Todd White, the evangelist known for healing, who prayed for 900 people before one of them was ever healed? What do you think happened between numbers 900 and 901? As he will tell you, he began to read in scripture about the Holy Spirit and became convinced he needed to receive this baptism.

One day he was able to go to a healing conference where a man from the stage singled Todd out of a room full of hundreds of people. He said, "You've been praying to receive the Holy Spirit, haven't you?" Todd responded in the affirmative and the man on the stage prayed, "Receive the Holy Spirit!" Suddenly Todd's knees buckled, and he fell to the ground groaning. He later recalled the experience was slightly painful. He was calling out for someone to help him. The preacher told everyone that he'd live, and went on with the service. That same week Todd experienced at least three miracles, including his first healing of a man in public suffering from a busted spine.

One morning, during our church's worship time, the Holy Spirit came upon me. It started small and sweet. I placed my hands out as if I was receiving a gift and began to feel light and tingly as I communed with Him. Several songs in, this feeling developed into a heaviness and *electricity*. The skin on my hands began to feel like it was being pricked, and it felt like jolts of power were rushing down my arms through the tips of my fingers. By the end of worship the electricity in my arms and hands turned painful, and I began to feel faint. I tried standing up, and I barely had enough consciousness to tell my wife, "I feel like I'm about to pass out, can you pray for me?" She prayed that I would be strengthened, and I was, but my arms continued to shake as if they were fully-charged battery cells.

People were called to the altar at this point. I looked up and saw two men kneeling down praying fervently. I knew in my heart I needed to touch them. I shuffled to the front, still under the weight of the Spirit, and put my hand on the shoulder of the first man. Immediately he broke down and began to weep. I then did the same for the second man. I prayed for both of them.

To this day I will feel the prickles on my hands as I go about my business. It comes and goes, and is a constant reminder that God's power is with me, and that I'm called to steward it rather than squander it.

A man cannot heal another person miraculously, but a man or woman with the Holy Spirit living inside of them, who has been clothed in power by

God through a baptism of the Spirit, will be able to do anything. As Reinhard Bonnke is fond of saying, "We have omnipotence at our fingertips." Let me tell you about one particular miracle that God used to stir faith in my entire church - leading many to be baptized in the Spirit and fire.

Chapter 6
"James! God healed my hand!"

It was an ordinary evening at Fairendell (the name my wife and I gave to our home). Friends were chatting while Aly cooked dinner. A dish in a pot needed to be warmed up, so Aly placed the whole pot in the hot oven. Time passed, and I went to the restroom while everyone else hung out in the kitchen. As I left the bathroom, I found my wife running cold water over her hand in great pain. She had absentmindedly grabbed the pot in the oven by the handle, *without a glove,* to take it out. The oven was at 5oo degrees, so it instantly seared her flesh.

She was doing everything she could to treat it - placing ice on it, lathering it in burn cream, etc. Her hand would go in and out of severe pain for the next couple of hours as she kept placing it under cold water and replacing the burn cream. Eventually, Aly started a habit she should not have - she'd put burn cream on her hand and then blow on it.

This had the effect of a person licking their chapped lips and blowing on them; it made the problem worse. Soon that was the only way she could find relief, and by nightfall, when it was time to crawl into bed, the pain overcame her.

My wife began to scream in agony. I had not heard her scream like that since a nurse pressed hard on her fresh c-section incision at the hospital years earlier. Except, that was just a *moment* of pain, but this pain would not go away. I went to take a shower, and as I often find myself doing, I got down on my knees and prayed to God. I wondered why Aly did not ask me to pray for her hand. We had seen only a few miracles at this point, but still - we *had* seen them!

Eventually, I decided I did not care if she didn't ask me; I would pray for her anyway. I toweled off, dressed for the night, and went to pray for her. I had a remarkable amount of joy and faith despite the situation. I got down on my knees and commanded her hand to be healed in the name of Jesus. I then prayed a little in tongues (I'll show you scripturally what this gift is, in a later chapter). Aly kept on screaming in pain - there was no instantaneous

healing, no warm feeling, and no tingles. I resolved
to get Nyquil to knock her out so she could at least
sleep. On my way to the medicine cabinet, a foolish
amount of faith came over me. I spoke to God, "I do
not care what I hear, I do not care what I see; she is
healed." I said this over and over like a chant, returned to give the Nyquil to my wife, and we both
laid down for bed. I put on soaking music (gentle
music we often play when we pray together) and
continued to pray over her while stroking her hair -
waiting for the medicine to kick in and put her to
sleep. Aly would later tell me she prayed herself that
night, "Jesus, if you gave the leper new skin, I believe you can do the same for me."

Morning came, and Aly was still asleep. I got out of
bed and went to feed our chickens out back. As I
returned, I heard my wife scream "James!" from our
bathroom across the house. "James!" she yelled
again as I remembered her hand, and a gloomy
thought crept into my mind. To my surprise, Aly
came running into the kitchen to meet me. "James!
God healed my hand! He healed my hand!" she exclaimed through tears. I knew this was a huge miracle, so I grabbed my phone and snapped pictures of
my wife ugly-crying while staring down at her hand

in awe. She would not stop going on about it!

I remember talking to my pastor once about how disappointed I was when people were miraculously healed and failed to worship God. I've since come to realize they do this for several reasons. Many of them will go home and privately break down in worship of the Lord - their personalities keep them from being overjoyed in public. Some of them are in such amazement they enter a state of shock. Others are faced with something they did not believe was possible, and the reality of it demolishes their prior assumptions concerning the Holy Spirit; they need time to digest it. I've noticed that this final group will become contemplative for a long time - sometimes talking themselves out of belief.

My pastor reminded me that this lack of exuberance upon being healed isn't anything new. He referred to a time in the bible when Jesus healed ten lepers, and only one turned around to worship Christ for what He had done (Luke 17). Be careful, friend. The enemy will come to steal the word almost immediately when the Spirit has moved. Do not give our enemy an inch in your life, do not let him steal your joy and praise.

On this day, my wife was the one leper who turned back to praise God. News of this miracle spread quickly as Aly recorded a testimony video and published it on social media. She also preached the good news to anyone who would hear her that day - to the doctor who had seen her the night before and diagnosed her with second-degree burns, to our neighbors, and even to one of her clients who wasn't a Christian.

I researched how long it takes to heal from second-degree burns and found it can be up to twenty-one days. What God did was indeed a miracle. We had photographs to prove it because my wife took a picture of her burned hand the night before, and in that photo you can see the skin splitting open all over. She then took a photo the following morning; it was new beautiful skin.

Neither of us could imagine what this miracle would do to people who heard about it. I think people can say a lot of things about Aly and I - our life is chaotic, we are strong-willed, and our politics aren't kosher - but I think one thing God has convicted many people of is the fact that we are not liars. You can say many things about the Thayers, but I don't believe anyone could levy an accusation of dishonesty. Thus, this miracle proved to be a stumbling block to some (I lost more Instagram followers that day than any other in my life after posting about this miracle), but for others, it stirred their faith.

That Sunday, our pastors surprised us when they asked Aly and I to come on stage and tell the audience about what happened. We jointly gave the testimony from each of our perspectives, after which pastor Joel Ramsey asked me to pray for everyone's healing in the audience that needed it. I had never done this before - I was used to praying for people individually. But the Holy Spirit stirred great boldness in me, and I began to lift up all those people who had their hands raised high to receive healing.

I told them what it cost for them to receive healing - the terrible death Jesus endured. I said, "I firmly believe the only reason Aly's hand is healed is because Jesus' were pierced." I commanded their bodies to be healed in the name of Jesus and then I began to, embarrassingly, weep. I was overcome with the thought of my own testimony and began to praise God for freeing me from depression so many years ago. I asked Him to do it again for those in the audience. I finally finished praying what was on my heart, and guess what? About 4 or 5 people were instantly and miraculously healed - testifying to the fact immediately after the prayer. I stepped out of the boat again, in a big way, and God did not let me sink. He is faithful, friend.

You may think this story would end there, but not by a long shot. The service continued, and pastor Savannah Ramsey stepped up to preach, but she could not. All morning she had been in prayer, and Holy Spirit continued to tell her He had different plans for the day than the ones she had prepared. Savannah moves in the prophetic heavily, and in a way I'm honestly a little frightened to ask God for. She sees things in the Spirit that you and I may not see. For example, one time she and I were praying for a woman together and Savannah said she could see knives sticking out of this lady's back. Sure enough, this woman said she had terrible pain in her spine caused by disease. Savannah then goes to, quite literally, remove these knives only she can see.

Another time she was praying for a young man in our church and she could see, in the Spirit, chains wrapped around his body. Savannah decided to take the chains off, and suddenly the man started to manifest a demon. On that same topic, one time she was traveling with her husband who happened to be in a very irritable mood. He recalls that she flicked his shoulder a little and instantly felt better. He asked what on Earth she did, to which she responded, "There was a little demon crawling on your shoulder, so I flicked it off."

And to add one more story concerning myself: Remember when I told you about the time I was in church and the Holy Spirit came upon me with power that felt like electricity? Later, Savannah told me she saw lightning come out of my hand and into that first man I touched at the altar.

If you knew where Savannah came from, how she was once separated from her husband for about 1.5 years, bound by Satan in depression and anxiety, and losing her mind - you'd understand why she walks so powerfully in the Spirit. God freed her from that spiritual sickness and miraculously reconciled her husband to her (he received a vision from God which spurred him to repent and reconcile). So when Savannah starts to talk about the Holy Spirit,

I sit up and listen. I listen with all my heart because I want to know Him as well as she knows Him.

On this day, He told her to throw away the sermon she planned. Savannah was obedient to this and just stood on stage waiting. Finally, the Spirit gave her words to preach - and they were all about Him. She introduced this third Person of the Trinity, telling us about His personality and character. Then she asked my wife to come on stage again. Savannah said the hand-healing miracle was not a coincidence and related it to a past anecdote. She asked people to come down to the altar to receive the Holy Spirit - and had Aly pray for us.

Friend, I ran. I was the very first person down there. I may have been the man with faith to pray for my wife's healing, but I knew I was just a man. I wanted more of the Spirit. In scripture you will find the Holy Spirit comes upon the disciples repeatedly. I once counted at least three times in a single chapter of Acts that these people were filled with the Spirit of God. Often the phrase used is, "X, filled with the Spirit..." or "The Spirit came upon X."

The truth is, you will never be fully satisfied with your level of intimacy with God or the amount of infilling of the Spirit you've received. I believe we'll always crave more until we're fully satiated in the next life. As it stands, I take any opportunity to be repeatedly baptized in the Spirit of God. I need Him so much; I am nothing without Him.

I knelt at the altar, and someone came around to anoint us with oil. You should know that oil in the bible is symbolic of the Holy Spirit. According to the book of James, elders of a church are supposed to anoint sick people with oil, and if they pray in faith, the ill person will be healed (James 5). I do not know why Holy Spirit acknowledges the use of oil. There is nothing magical about olive oil, but when we apply it to someone in faith and obedience, the Holy Spirit is *faithful* to move.

A bit of oil was pressed on my forehead, and I began to weep. I told God I wanted more of Him. I boldly told Him I would not leave until He blessed me. I was thinking of Jacob in the bible, who wrestles with the Lord and refuses to let Him go until he is blessed (Genesis 32:26).

The Holy Spirit fell on our entire church that day (see Acts 10:44). Many were laid out on the ground, convicted of their sins, and healed. I was so caught up in what God was doing to me that I can't comment on everyone else's experience, so I'll tell you mine.

I've come to jokingly refer to this type of experience as being "sat on by the Holy Spirit." There are times when He comes upon you with such glory that the weight of it makes it difficult to stand in His presence. I wanted to give in, so I just laid on the floor. Then, He began to show me something. It was like I was seeing all the people Jesus died to heal that I would pray for. It was overwhelming. There were just so many of them. Then I sensed what Jesus underwent to procure their healing - an awful beating and death on a cross. My mind broke. I just kept saying "How?, How?, How?" The Lord so overcame me that I could not even verbalize the complete sentence of what I was asking.

I was trying to ask Him, "How could you love them that much?" I wanted to know how Jesus could love this massive multitude of people He would heal through me - to endure that heinous cross. It seemed so horrible; it seemed insurmountable. Why would Jesus love us that much? I felt broken. I felt humbled. And the Lord, in His grace, gave me an answer. He said, "You do not need to know how; you just need to know it is true."

Friend, every gift of the Spirit is activated out of love. Remember that! Jesus and the Father deeply love the person you pray for to be healed or freed. Christ placed tremendous suffering upon Himself so this person in front of you might be healed. God the Father loves this person in front of you to death - literally to the death of His Son. If you have children, you know you would not give one of them up to save another person - not even a good person. Yet God gave up His Son for the ungodly and sinners like you and me (Romans 5:8). It is out of this great love that we come to people with broken hearts and broken bodies and undo the damage our enemy has caused. Jesus is worthy to receive His reward for His suffering.

Still lying on the floor, I asked God to explain something. I reminded Him that I was once in this spot before - twenty-ish years ago when He took my depression from me. I reminded Him that He had given me two visions, and I asked Him to provide me with revelation concerning them. He then told me what one of them meant. When I was ten years old, lying on the floor of that church, one of the things I saw was a pyramid made from stone blocks. One of the blocks had lots of cracks in it, and it was that block which drew all of my attention. This made no sense to me for twenty years. In hindsight, if God had explained it before I began to walk in miracles, I probably would not have had a grid to understand it anyway - so He chose His timing well. He told me, "People are cracked. Their hearts are cracked, and their bodies are cracked. You will heal them." I just wept.

From here, I must qualify a statement I made previously. I wrote to you that I did not have to pray for nearly as many people as Shane or Todd did before I started to see miracles. This statement may be untrue, depending on how you view it. But, the truth is, I've prayed for the sick since I can remember. For decades I'd be driving my car, or walking around town, seeing people with broken bodies, and I'd lift them up in a quick prayer, "God, if it is your will, please heal that person." I've probably prayed for thousands of people this way.

But can I tell you this is not how Christ has called

us to pray for people? In the next chapter, I will explain some deep theology on this subject that we need to start embracing if our churches are ever going to burn bright in this dark world again.

I want to end *this* chapter by returning to Aly's burned hand. God took a tiny miracle like that, and He used it as a vehicle to heal many more and stir the faith of dozens to receive the Holy Spirit. Months later, testimonies still rolled in spurred on by this miracle.

A couple at our church said they were first time visitors the Sunday we shared our testimony of healing - and that *it* was the reason they decided to stay. A woman told my wife that she had shared the miracle with her mother - whose heart had grown quite cold towards truth and the Lord - and that it caused her to weep at the thought, "God still does miracles!"

Never underestimate the power of a testimony to change the hearts of men. It is called a "testimony" because it is repeatable. If God did it in one person's life, He could do it in another's. We are called to be lamps in the world, and Jesus would admonish us if we hid those lamps under a basket (Matthew 5). If

God heals you, please tell anyone you can because you never know who else is depending on your testimony to receive their own miracle. Be the one leper that came back to Jesus.

Chapter 7
Your Authority in Christ

Take everything you believe about the miraculous, whether God still moves today, and set it aside for a moment. I want to take you back to scripture because for too long we've allowed man-made doctrines to guide our hearts on this matter, and I believe God is pointing us back to His word as our final authority instead.

First, can we talk about what scripture does not say concerning the gifts of the Spirit? It demonstrably does not say they ended with the apostles, nor does it say (and how could it, logically speaking?) they ended with the canonization of scripture itself. Nor do we find in scripture that only the twelve disciples worked miracles like healing. These are all false myths. Try as hard as you might, you will find no such things as these spoken about in scripture. The only point at which the gifts cease, that scripture clearly lays out (1 Corinthians 13), is when Christ returns. At this point, something like healing will have no use because, as Revelation 21 tells us, no one will be sick. At this point, something like prophecy will have no use because we will have complete knowledge.

The history of the doctrine of Cessationism (that the gifts of the Spirit have ceased and are no longer in operation today) is a sad one. John Calvin, one of the great reformers of the Protestant Reformation, was breaking from the Catholic church. Meanwhile, the Catholic church at the time was proclaiming miracles in the church itself. To demonize Catholicism, Calvin created the formal doctrine of Cessationism. This belief has been passed down to many denominations of Christianity, and as such, the Holy Spirit has been discarded.

Note that John Calvin did not come to believe this doctrine based on scriptural evidence (which is ironic, as the Reformers were all about deriving doctrine from scripture alone). Instead, he created it based on experiential wisdom (not seeing healing come from the "laying on of hands" anymore) using unrighteous motives (demonizing his opposition). I have found today that the majority of people who do not believe God still does miracles are this way because of one of two reasons:

1. Because their family or church has incorpo-
   rated this doctrine and passed it down to
   them.

2. Because they have never seen a miracle before.

These two reasons are boiled down to a mere lack
of experience with the miraculous - whether by the
adherent of the doctrine of Cessationism or by
those who passed it down to them.

It may be an *experientially* derived doctrine, but it is
not *scriptural*, and I have yet to find a single person
who even attempts to argue otherwise because
scripture leaves us zero evidence for it. So what
does the bible have to tell us concerning our ability
to heal the sick?

Let me start with the words of Jesus. We find in
Matthew 10 that Jesus sends out His twelve disciples
to the Jewish people. In verse eight, He commands
them to "heal the sick, raise the dead, cleanse the
lepers, [and] drive out demons." The disciples leave

to do these things. Many Christians like to stop here and say, "Well, that's great for the people that walked with Jesus, but that's not for me." In that case, let's keep going for a moment.

Jesus' ministry grows and in Luke 10 He sends out seventy-two of His followers, not just the Twelve, and commands them to "heal the sick" in verse nine. At this point the Christian may be tempted to say, "Well, that's just seventy-two people, and Jesus was still alive; surely this does not apply to me!" Let's continue.

After Christ died and rose again, and after Pentecost, we find a man named Philip whom I've discussed previously. Philip was not an apostle but is referred to as an evangelist - someone who preaches the gospel. We see in Acts 8 that Philip drove demons out of people, and they were miraculously healed. We find the Holy Spirit gave him the boldness to preach and even teleported him somewhere (keep in mind, God is omnipresent)! This man did not physically walk with Jesus that we know of, and he did not have a radical experience with Him like Paul did on the road to Damascus.

Philip was a regular believer - a guy who kept saying "yes" to the Lord when he had an opportunity. His story starts with him doing administrative work; he then heals a ton of people, drives demons out, boldly proclaims the gospel, and in the end, we find out he had four daughters who had the gift of prophecy in Acts 21:9. Were these daughters part of the Twelve? The seventy-two? No way! These were regular followers of Jesus who had an earthly father full of the Spirit of God. It would not surprise me if Philip laid hands on his daughters to receive the Holy Spirit.

I've brought up Mark 16 before, but I want to focus on one particular promise to drive this point home. Jesus tells us what sort of signs would follow those who believed in Him: "In my name they will drive out demons; they will speak in new tongues; they will pick up snakes with their hands; and when they drink deadly poison, it will not hurt them at all; they will place their hands on sick people, and they will get well." Notice the language. He didn't say these signs will follow "the 12 apostles" or "those who live during the Roman Era" or "those who live before the canonization of scripture." He said, these signs will follow those who *believe.*

The Holy Spirit is for every believer. In Acts 2, Peter stands up to give his first bold sermon after being empowered by the Spirit. He proclaims that the prophecy of Joel has come to pass, "And it will be in the last days, says God, that I will pour out my Spirit on **all** people; then your sons and your daughters will prophesy, your young men will see visions, and your old men will dream dreams."

Later in Acts, we find that even the apostles are shocked (and excited) to learn that the Holy Spirit was coming upon gentiles (non-Jews). I want you to know from this section that you are not barred from doing the miraculous by any category. Whether you're ethnically Jew, gentile, male, female, old, young, etc. God's Spirit has been poured out for you. Please don't ignore Him!

I mentioned the seventy-two that Christ sent out previously. We know they went out to heal the sick and preach the gospel, but they came back with a grand revelation: "The seventy-two returned with joy and said, "Lord, even the demons submit to us in your name." [Jesus] replied, 'I saw Satan fall like lightning from heaven. I have given you authority to trample on snakes and scorpions and to overcome all the power of the enemy; nothing will harm you."

Did you catch it? Christ gave them *authority*.

One of the first miracles I witnessed after Kevin's shoulder was healed in church was that of a demon-possessed man set free. This man had come to a bonfire we hosted at Fairendell one night and liked some of the people he met from our church. Shortly after, he said he wanted to come to church some-time - and of course I was all about that. Little did I know how insanely difficult it would be to get him there.

Curiously, this man had a propensity for injuring himself anytime he came over. He'd step out of his vehicle on solid flat ground and rip his toe open. We'd be ready to sit at my dining room table to dis-cuss the gospel, and he'd tear a massive gash in his kneecap. On two separate occasions he accidentally almost killed himself at my house, even!

There were other strange things about this man too. We'd be in conversation about something or anoth-er, and he'd suddenly forget what we were talking about. Whenever we discussed anything serious concerning the Lord, his memory would phase in and out. For example, he'd reveal to me that he had thought about killing himself and then demand to know who told me that fact, not sixty seconds later.

I eventually became absurdly frustrated with trying to minister to him. When I preached any bit of truth, he'd forget it almost instantly or be distracted by something else - even though simultaneously he'd tell me that he wanted to hear about it. When we'd invite him to church, he would honestly try to come, but every single time something would keep him from showing up.

One night this friend was over at my house as usual. We were sitting at my kitchen bar, my little girls were playing around our feet, and my wife was washing dishes. Off the cuff, my friend asked me if I'd ever heard of a specific (he named it) demon before. I told him "No." I then looked into his eyes and could see the demon inside him. I asked him, "Am I talking to (insert name of demon) right now?" He stared back at me with a tight smile as if trying to pierce my soul. His upper lip quivered. Suddenly, my eldest daughter began what would become one of the loudest and wildest temper tantrums she'd ever had (she was roughly four years old at this time). I was about to attempt to drive this demon out of my friend, something I had never really done before, when I realized that it may put my family in danger.

I changed the subject and prepared my daughters for bed, but I knew I couldn't let this go on any longer. I've heard it said that the moment Satan shows himself, it is time to deal with him. You see, demons do not want to be seen. The bible says our bodies can be homes for them (Matthew 12). They do not want to leave their homes, so their best bet is to convince people they do not exist and especially to keep themselves hidden from the Holy Spirit's power - all effective armies use camouflage.

In the bible we find about a third of Jesus' miracles involved driving out demons. On a specific occasion, Jesus was driving a demon out when a man began to proclaim that Jesus must drive out demons by the power of a demon. I love that the Lord responds by pointing out the logical inconsistency in that argument - "A house divided against itself cannot stand" (Matthew 12). In reality, though, Jesus said He drove demons out by the Finger of God - or the Holy Spirit. Would it surprise you to know that demons are absolutely terrified of the Holy Spirit? I mean, you and I do not know fear in comparison. We genuinely don't. Demons know fear though; they will do anything they can to not come up against the Finger of God. The book of James says they "shudder" at the thought of God. On one occasion, demons *begged* Jesus not to send them into "the abyss."

Popular culture likes to make these entities out to be big baddies that can't be resisted. Don't get me wrong, they are evil - entirely twisted by probably billions or trillions of years worth of traveling down a dark rebellious path - but they are nothing compared to God. They are like parasites clinging to anyone that will let them stick around. Jesus said that hell was originally created for "Satan and his angels" (Matthew 25) who existed long before mankind. These unclean spirits know their time is limited, that one day Jesus will return and cast them into the lake of fire. They live in terror of that day, and during the present age they are afraid someone with the Holy Spirit inside of them will send them there before the appointed time.

One note I want to make is demons are more prevalent than people tend to think, and just because a person is oppressed by one doesn't mean that person is sinful or evil. It means they are bound and need Jesus to free them - like a sick person who needs Jesus to heal them. In both cases, *if* personal sin caused the predicament, Jesus would tell that person to repent and stop sinning (John 5:14) right after healing them.

If demons don't want to be caught, why would this one tell me its name? Do you recall the man possessed by a legion of demons in Mark 5? Jesus is a long way off from this man when he comes running up to Him, falls at His feet, and the demons inside of him begin to negotiate terms with Jesus. Something about the Spirit of God brings these things to the surface in people. The presence of God is torture to them, which is why sometimes when you pray for the sick, you'll find the person in front of you begin to manifest a demon. They've been hidden for so long, but the power and presence of the Holy Spirit inside you begins to push them to a breaking point. Their moment of discovery has arrived, and they frequently throw temper tantrums at this point or try to scare you into backing down, or they'll feign leaving. They have many tactics to throw us off the case, but Jesus has commanded us to drive them out, so we must try.

After getting my children into bed that night, I texted pastor Joel, "Hey, a demon in this man just told me its name (I sent a Wikipedia article about this specific demon). Do you want to come over and help me drive it out?" He agreed to come over and do just that. So I returned to my friend and persuaded him that we should play video games. He was a little on edge but allowed me to pop some Mario Kart 64 in. Eventually, I decided it would be weird for my pastor to show up unannounced, so I told my friend that Joel was headed over.

Immediately he became terrified. He asked me over and over again, "Are you serious? Is he really coming over? Don't lie to me James! He isn't really coming over!" I knew this was the *thing* inside my friend talking, expressing concern. I assured him that my pastor was headed over, and to trick the spirit I told him he was coming to play video games with us. The demon was not fooled.

My buddy called pastor Joel and asked if he was really headed over - which my pastor confirmed. My friend then asked Joel to stop and pick up some beer to bring with him, to which my pastor said he was bringing wine. This confused my friend, so my pastor clarified, "I'm bringing *new wine*." I cracked up laughing (on the inside).

In Mark 2, Jesus gives us an image of what it is like to be filled with the Holy Spirit. He says that no one puts new wine in an old wineskin (a container for wine made from leathered animal skin); why? Because the wineskin will burst open. Instead, He says that new wine must be poured into new wineskins. When you become a Christian, you are what the bible calls a "new creation." You are "reborn," not of the flesh or the will of man, but of the Spirit (John 1:13). You become a new wineskin. This must occur so you can become a vessel for the Holy Spirit.

The "New Wine" is the Holy Spirit. If He took residence in an "old wineskin," or someone who was not reborn of the Spirit through Christ, then the implication is they would die. This makes sense because we're told that even to look at God would cause us to die (Exodus 33:20) - that the Father dwells in unapproachable light. Apart from Christ, we are not made of the kind of stuff that can be as near to a Holy God as we become when the Spirit fills us.

I like to give the illustration of our Sun, which burns at almost six-thousand degrees Kelvin. If we were to launch a probe into the Sun, it would inevitably be crushed and burned up - it just isn't made of suitable material to withstand the Sun's heat (or gravity). Similarly, God's holiness is too great for sinful man to bear the fullness of His presence. As such, we must have the atonement of Jesus applied to our lives so we can become righteous and therefore made of the "right stuff" to experience the fullness of God. Pastor Joel, being a new creation, was full of the New Wine, or the Holy Spirit. He was taunting the demon inside my friend.

My pastor hung up, and my friend came back inside. He looked at my wife and I with terror in his eyes and said, "James, if I leave here and Joel shows up, you have to promise me you'll come get me and bring me back!" This was my friend speaking, not the demon; My friend wanted freedom. Eventually, my pastor did show up and was *warmly* greeted by my friend with a, "Why are you here!?"

We all sat down in the living room, and Joel began to pour into this man as he and I had been doing for months. We encouraged him about his life - the things God had planned for him and how loved he was. The demon did not like this and eventually came to the surface. He started yelling at Joel, "I'm not afraid of you! I'm not afraid of you!" and became aggressive.

Joel then moved closer to my friend on the couch. We all encouraged him a little more (my wife was there, too), and then my friend uttered a very eerie phrase.

"We are ten thousand," he said as he rolled his head around. I thought to myself, "Oh man, it is go time!" but my pastor asked, "What did you just say?" Then he looked into my friend's eyes and could see the demon much like I did earlier in the day. He put his hand on my friend's chest and began to drive the demon out. I ran over to my friend, put my hand on his knee, and began to pray, but primarily I just watched and learned because I had never done a deliverance (others use the word "exorcism") before - nothing like *that*, anyway.

When all was said and done, about twenty minutes later, roughly five or six demons had come out of my friend that I could tell. When the final one came out (a spirit of infirmity), God simultaneously healed my friend of a disorder. He let out a large belch and breathed deeply. Previously my friend could not breathe out of one of his nostrils. He took a deep breath for the first time in three years.

The next day he told us that he had been having nightmares for months and that night was the first night he hadn't - he slept like a rock. The following morning he was shocked that even the grass seemed different. He no longer wanted to kill himself and no longer heard voices. I want to tell you how this event shaped my understanding of our authority in Christ.

I think many people may come away from such an experience a little freaked out, but I saw my pastor a few days later and told him what God had revealed to me through watching this deliverance. I hope I always remember the main thing I took away: the demons *had* to obey.

Sit there for a moment and understand how monumental this revelation is. Powerful beings created long before you and I were born, ones without material bodies who can manipulate matter nonetheless, ones who previously stood in the presence of almighty God, must obey you if you are in Christ. Remember what the seventy-two said when they came back, "Lord, even the demons submit to us in your name!" That revelation came upon me like a ton of bricks, and it significantly increased my faith.

The night I went to pray for my wife's hand to be healed, I thought back to this event. I told myself, "If even demons have to obey me, how much more do skin cells on a hand?" What authority we have in Jesus! Can I tell you that this is a humbling concept to come to terms with? I don't think I'll ever understand why Jesus trusts us with such power. Perhaps, like understanding how He could love people enough to suffer for their healing, I don't have to know the answer to this question. Maybe I just need to accept that it is true and walk on in that authority.

The bible calls us ambassadors for Christ (2 Corinthians 5:20). An ambassador represents a nation-state. He or she is vested with responsibilities to their nation, and given the power to engage in negotiations with enemies and allies. You are an ambassador for the most powerful kingdom ever to exist - and you've been sent from that kingdom by a great King, Jesus Christ, who has given you both a mission and authority to complete it. He said He gave us authority over every dark power in this world (Luke 10:19). As C.S. Lewis once remarked, "We live in enemy-occupied territory." According to the bible, Satan is considered the god of this world (2 Corinthians 4:4). We eat and play and worship in the middle of a warzone between our God's kingdom, which is invading, and the kingdom of darkness that stands here. We have been given a sword to wage war with.

That Sword is the Spirit of God - remember it is by the Finger of God we drive out demons. Thus, regarding how we operate in this war, the Trinity works as such: God the Father has a will that consists of saving souls. 2 Peter 3:9 says He wills all to come to repentance. It also includes, at the least, healing the sick, casting out demons, cleansing the leper, and raising the dead – all things Jesus told

His disciples to do.

The Son was handed all authority, and then He delegated a good deal of it to His body - the Church. We are His agents on Earth, His ambassadors. Yet, we are just men and women! How can we heal a broken body or drive out an unclean spirit? That's where God the Holy Spirit steps in, as I've previously asserted. He is the power of God. It was by the Holy Spirit that Christ was raised from the dead. It was by the Holy Spirit that the Red Sea parted, and by the Holy Spirit Jesus drove out demons. The *Father* wills us to do good works, we have been given authority to do them by *Jesus*, and we practically apply that authority through the power of the *Holy Spirit*.

An objection is often raised at this point. People think we presume upon God if we command healing. Do you remember me telling you about how I used to pray for the sick, "God, if it is your will, please heal this person?" Well, after Shane prayed for me that one night, and I resolved to pursue praying for the sick, I read through both Mark and Acts to see how people in the bible prayed for healing. What I discovered was shocking because no one I knew had taught it to me before. Almost every time the sick were prayed for, it was done by a command. The command would be something like, "Get up and walk," or "Be healed," or "Stretch out your hand." The person praying would literally command this other person's body to do something.

I want you to remember that even though we've been given authority, we are likewise under authority. Jesus *expected* us to heal the sick - it is plain as day in scripture. We aren't waiting on Him to tell us His will. He already told it to us! Unfortunately, many Christians, who have been given authority to heal the sick and commanded by their King to do so, are still putzing around waiting for God to "reveal His will" for sick people. They ask themselves, "Does God want this person to be healed?" Leaving the option open makes them double-minded. Like James said in James 1:6, such people ask and don't believe they'll receive anything - so they don't.

When we ask God to do something, we must believe He wills to do it. If you think there's a chance He does not want to do something, then you do not believe He wills to do it.

A couple of friends, my wife, and myself have started to put on Freedom Nights at Fairendell. These are events where we invite anyone and everyone to come out, worship God in our living room, and receive prayer. The first one of these saw five or six miracles, but one stood out to me.

A man showed up whom I had met previously on a film set. On that set, I told my testimony to a group he was part of. At the end, he said something to the effect of, "Can you go back and tell me again what took your depression away?" He revealed to me that since his teenage years, he had been struggling with depression and suicidality. I asked him several questions about more practical things, such as whether he felt he was doing meaningful work and had a purpose in life. These weren't his issues. Eventually, I said, "I know there are a lot of people here that may not want to talk about such things, but I have to tell you that what you're dealing with is demonic. You need someone to pray for you to rid you of your depression like someone did for me."

Sometimes I must override decorum, put my reputation on the line, and play the part of the fool because the Holy Spirit wants to do something for someone. This was a group of strangers; I had only met one of the six men before this day. I was risking my job and risking being branded as the weirdo that talks about demons.

Yet the Holy Spirit knows what He is doing. It was this seed that kept this man's curiosity peaking. He found himself at my house for our first Freedom Night, readily admitting he had no idea why he was there. He sat in the back, ignoring each call to prayer, watching person after person find healing or freedom. Finally, at the very end, he came up for prayer - but he was double-minded.

He said he believed God *could* free him, but he didn't know if God *wanted* to, and if He would do it tonight or another day. I told him that tonight was his night and that we would not ask God for something we did not believe we'd receive. So we all laid hands on him and prayed. My wife received a word of knowledge for him, and he began to cry upon hearing it. Suddenly, the two worship leaders heard from God that they should play a specific song, and so they did. We kept praying and some of us were singing when suddenly this man lifted his head and opened his mouth. He began to worship God - loudly and unapologetically! He then stood up and cried, "God has freed me; I'm healed!"

I saw that man a Sunday later, and he was smiling from ear to ear. It remains one of the most beautiful miracles I have ever witnessed.

Friends, get the question of whether or not God wants to heal or deliver people out of your head. Jesus healed every person that came to Him for it. Can you imagine putting this doctrine in His mouth? A sick person comes to Jesus and says, "Please heal me!" to which Jesus responds, "I would, but I don't want to." That isn't our Lord! Our Lord came to "sozo" us.

Sozo is the Greek word we often translate into "save" in scripture. The word means "save, heal, deliver, and restore (make whole)." It is a complete package. God desires our salvation from our sins, our healing from sickness, our deliverance from evil, and our restoration from past trauma. He is a good God, and He has commanded us to heal the sick. He would not command it if He did not will it, and He would not give us authority to do it if He did not desire to see us use that authority.

Pastor Joel once summed up this double-minded way of thinking like this: "Imagine I sent you to the store to buy something for me, and I gave you my credit card so you could complete the transaction. Now pretend after you got there, you called me on the phone and asked if I wanted you to buy the thing I sent you to buy. Do you not see how silly that sounds? Of course I want you to buy it! I sent you with explicit instructions to purchase it, and I also gave you the money to purchase it with."

The authority we have in Christ is beyond our imagination. In John 14:12, Jesus tells us that we would do the same things He did, and even greater ones, because He would be returning to the Father (and thus He would send us the Holy Spirit). Jesus did a lot of amazing things - the Man raised the dead for goodness sake! He promises us that we can too. You may have read where Jesus tells His disciples that if they even have a little faith, they can say to a mountain to move, and it must move? Have you also read where He said if we had even a bit of faith we could tell a tree to uproot itself and be planted in the ocean (Luke 17:6)? Do you believe Him?

I believe Him. I sincerely do because of a specific

experience I had praying for a man. It was a Sunday morning, and I was late getting to the Biblical Foundations class I teach at church. I whipped into the parking lot and hopped out. I was racing to get inside when an older man caught my eye. He struggled to get out of his vehicle, which was parked in the handicapped zone. I watched him limp toward the door far behind me, wincing in pain as he went along. The thought crossed my mind, "Wouldn't it be great if one day the church didn't need handicap parking spaces because everyone was healed?" I went to my class.

Five minutes later, that same older man hobbled into my classroom. He mistakenly thought it was the Seniors Life Group. As he was walking out, I asked him about his ailment, "Is it something wrong with your spine or hips?" He responded, "No, I have large kidney stones in my right kidney. I had the ones in my left kidney removed already. The pain makes it difficult to walk." I asked him if we could pray for him, to which he agreed and sat down in a chair.

I had my students lay hands on him, and I began to pray, "God, thank you for this man whom you love.

He is your son. I lift him up to you now." I then opened my eyes and spoke to his body, "Kidney stones, I command you to dissolve right now in the name of Jesus Christ! Pain leave!" The prayer took a total of sixty seconds. I then asked the man to stand up and test it. He responded, "I felt it in my side." He then got up from the chair and began to walk around the room. He became excited (as much as a man his age could display) and exclaimed, "Oh, it feels so good to be able to walk without pain!" He praised God and thanked us as he left the room.

It wasn't until later that night Jesus' words hit me - "You can say to this mountain 'move,' and it will move." I thought about the kidney stones and decided to do some research. I discovered that they are literal rocks - mostly made from calcium. It was then I determined I must take Jesus at His word, for I had said to those rocks to be dissolved, and they were dissolved. Jesus had given me authority over even the elements in His name.

I will share two more brief stories to drive home this point on just how much authority you have in Christ. The first is not my own, but that of a friend - and the whole thing was caught on video. This friend was ministering in a third-world nation. He often prays for the sick. In fact, that's pretty much what his little ministry is known for. There was a person with terrible back pain whom he endeavored to pray for. Unfortunately, one of the legs on this person was shorter than the other, causing them to walk unevenly and thus creating the pain.

My friend laid this person on their back and brought their feet together. Sure enough, one leg was shorter than the other. He then commanded the short leg to grow - and it grew! At first, it grew very slowly, so my friend kept telling it "more, more, more" until, at one point, that leg was now longer than the other. This was not great, so he then commanded it to go back a little until they were aligned - and it did.

The second story has a similar moral, which I'll explain shortly. I was asked to pray for a friend suffering from debilitating fear and an inability to sleep at night. This would eventually be a failed deliverance on my part, for although the man felt the presence of God and I was even able to give him a word of knowledge, I failed to drive the demon out. Part of that failure came from not recognizing what I was dealing with, and the other part was exercising my authority over pain to our disadvantage. In the middle of praying, my friend told me he had significant pain in his chest that came on when we started. I did not know then what I know now - that this is often a demon manifesting itself under the weight of the Holy Spirit. So instead of going in hard and driving the demon out, I prayed the pain would leave, and it did.

Think about these two stories for a moment. In both cases, the person praying used their authority over sickness, but in such a way that it was detrimental to the right outcome - a leg too long, a pain indicating a deeper issue, brushed off. The lesson here is to use wisdom when exercising your authority in Christ, but it is also to reflect in awe at what Jesus has handed you to wage war against the demonic powers of our world and the effects of sin.

There is one more misconception I want to clear up before moving on. We are told to pray "in the name of Jesus," and you'll frequently hear Christians end their prayers with the specific words, "In the name of Jesus, I pray, amen." This is not what it means to pray in the name of Jesus. It is not about the words we use but about what we pray for.

John 14:13 is where Jesus tells us that if we ask for anything in His name, He will do it. That bold and absolute statement confuses many people because they don't know what it means to ask in the name of Christ. As I've written several times, we are Jesus' representatives. Whenever we enter a dark situation, we come in His name to do the same things He did. These are things in the character of Christ such as casting out demons, healing the sick, cleansing the leper, raising the dead, or preaching the good news. In context, the prior verses let us know this statement is all about the works of Jesus. These are the types of things that Jesus guarantees us He'll do if we remain in Him.

Are you praying for a million dollars to enrich yourself in the name of Jesus? Not really - it isn't in His character; you're fooling yourself. But if you're praying for a sick person to be healed, then that is praying in the name of Jesus. Imagine yourself like a king's herald of old. You arrive at a foreign court and speak, "In the name of my king, I have come to deliver a message and to do his will!" That is what it means to pray in the name of Jesus. The thing you are saying and the thing you are doing must be in accordance with the character of Jesus - you are there in His name.

Chapter 8
How to Heal the Sick

This is probably the chapter you picked this book up for. I must tell you that at first you'll be disappointed, but if you bear with me a little while, I assure you I'll give several practical tips you can implement while praying for the sick. The first notion I must dispel is that there is a formula when it comes to God healing people. As frustrating as this may be to our minds, God healing people is closer to an art than to science. Healing offends the intellect - probably by design. There is no formula above and beyond the fact God does the healing, you do the praying, and either you or the person you're praying for - someone, anyone - must have the tiniest bit of faith.

I created a spreadsheet when I first endeavored to see the sick healed. In that spreadsheet, I kept track of data such as who I prayed for, the words I spoke, their problem, the result, and so forth. I was trying to figure out the formula for seeing the sick healed. However, the longer I kept tracking results, the less clear of a picture I could see. It honestly felt like the Holy Spirit was telling me to stop trying to put Him in a bottle.

In the gospels we find Jesus healed many people, but very rarely were two people ever healed the same way. One person had mud put on his blind eyes; another is told their sins are forgiven first (more on that later); a third is commanded to stretch their hand out; another is told nothing at all - she simply touches His cloak. When we get to the book of Acts, the miracles get even more peculiar - people are healed by the shadow of Peter or by touching a cloth from Paul.

I have a friend from church who recently started praying for the sick with success (he even prayed for a woman going blind, and she was healed!) One day he prayed for a deaf girl without immediate healing, and Satan put him under great condemnation the rest of the day. He confided in me that in the moment of praying he felt the same way he had felt before when people had been healed - a rush of love from the Father for the sick person. He did not understand why the deaf girl was not healed based on this past feeling being present when he prayed. I had to remind him of the difficult truth - a repeat feeling is just a feeling. It is ultimately walking by *sight* rather than belief.

I'm telling you, give up now trying to formulate the Holy Spirit. He is often described as a wind - we don't know where He comes from nor where He is going, and the same is true for those born of the Spirit (John 3:8). We have to go at this whole thing like little children. We must step out of the boat in faith rather than in formula.

I mentioned previously that we anoint the sick with oil which symbolizes the Holy Spirit. I have seen God instantly alleviate the suffering of someone after placing anointing oil on their head. I have also seen no discernible response from that mere act. I've commanded sickness to leave, and it has gone within thirty seconds. I have also prayed five times for the same woman for months and watched as she steadily came to health. Like my wife's hand, I've prayed for people to be healed, and they went to bed still broken but woke up whole the following day. There is no formula.

It is essential to, first and foremost, be led by the

Holy Spirit when we pray for the sick. He is omniscient, so He knows every issue. Occasionally He will let us in on what that issue may be, and we can move in the Spirit very powerfully to heal. Often, though, we must just trust that He knows what He is doing. The Holy Spirit is called the Paraclete in Greek. That word is translated as Helper or Advocate or Counselor. It was primarily used, when scripture was written, to describe a family attorney. Yet the literal translation of the word Paraclete means "one who comes alongside."

Jesus told us in John 16:7 that it was to our advantage He left us. Jesus isn't on Earth anymore; He currently sits at the right hand of the Father. He states that if He did not leave, He could not send the Paraclete to us. Are you picking up what He is laying down? What could be better than Jesus Christ in the flesh standing in your living room with you? Well, Jesus thought having the Holy Spirit come to us was better. He is our Guide, our Friend, and He never leaves us - even when we sin, which hurts Him most terribly. He's simultaneously like a raging tempest and like a child of innocence who will be grieved if you ignore Him. We are supposed to *commune* with the Holy Spirit; that means we talk to Him. I can recommend a book called "Good Morning Holy Spirit" by Benny Hinn if you want to get to know the Holy Spirit more intimately.

What I want you to know is this: He is right there. While reading this book, He is right there next to you. Sometimes you can feel Him inside of you, and sometimes He comes upon you in great power, but know that as you drive your car, cry your eyes out, and celebrate the joys of life, the Holy Spirit is right next to you. This was demonstrated to me most profoundly one day when I was invited to hand out fliers at a local college - advertising an evangelistic outreach going on later that week. My wife and I were walking around campus, engaging students about the event, when we came upon a campus ministry with a booth handing out drinks and snacks. I could not help but overhear a debate between a militant atheist and several young Christians.

If you had known me during my college days, you would have found a young man passionately devoted to apologetics. During those years of my life, I studied philosophy and theology voraciously. I then leveraged all of that knowledge to bring cutting arguments upon my opponents. I especially loved debating militant atheists (of which I read and studied their works too - my favorite being those of Christopher Hitchens). So, unsurprisingly, I was drawn to this discussion. I crept up to the circle of students and listened until I found a time to jump in. The young atheist was rapidly telling his life-story and fall from the Christian faith. He had issues with God's salvation (why didn't He create us all saved to begin with?) I asked him more about his grievances, and then in my usual way I gave him several explanations and counterarguments.

The Christian students were relieved to have me step in like this, but they'd soon be pushed past their comfort zone. I wasn't there to make anyone comfortable. People are going to hell, and I need them to know how much God doesn't want them to end up there.

I suddenly felt the Holy Spirit come upon me. I thought He was eager to perform a miracle right there on the sidewalk. I cut the conversation short and told the young atheist directly, "This is enough talk *about* God. Do you want me to *show* you Him?" He started to become very frazzled. How many militant atheists are given an opportunity like that? Here is a Christian that is guaranteeing a miracle to be performed to prove the existence of God. Instead of excitement (for if his worldview was correct, then failure to perform the miracle would only embolden him), he became incredibly nervous.

"Do you have any pain in your body?" I asked, trying to figure out what Holy Spirit wanted to do. He tried to change the subject, but I went on, "Do you suffer from depression or anxiety?" This man, who was already exhibiting an absurd amount of anxiety, instantly began to manifest this same spirit. His arms shook uncontrollably, his mouth froze up, and he tried very hard to formulate a sentence. Unfortunately, one of the Christian students was starting to take issue with a separate statement I had made. I got distracted and turned to her to explain myself. At that moment, as my wife recalls, the young atheist, whose face was now flushed red, literally ran away. I looked back up, and he was gone.

So what was the Holy Spirit doing at this time? He was showing His teeth. I felt like He was about to pounce on this little demon of anxiety tormenting the young man and gobble it whole. I have learned that the Holy Spirit loves to show off. He is just itching to do miracles, and He absolutely hates unclean spirits - He wrecks them if given the opportunity.

In my old Christian walk, I would have just stood there arguing with this man until one of us got bored, but with the Holy Spirit by my side, I did not have to. "You don't believe in God? Ok, let me introduce you to Him - He's literally right here!" Never forget that the Holy Spirit is right there beside you (even if you don't *feel* Him). He does not want you to sink when you step out of the boat. Seriously, it is in His nature to perform miracles. We say the Trinity has three Persons. Persons have personalities. The Holy Spirit has one, and the more you walk with Him, and the more you talk to Him, the more He is willing to reveal Himself to you. I can honestly say He has become my best Friend. Understand this, and when you pray for the sick, leave room for Him to guide you - He's your Captain. There may not be a formula for healing the sick, but that doesn't mean you're left in the dark.

Barring a word of knowledge given to me by the Holy Spirit, I almost always start praying for the sick by building their confidence in God's love for them. I want them to understand just how deep the Father's love is, how He has called them a son or daughter. I know other people who will start by regaling the sick person with stories of past miracles to build their faith, and I have done this on occasion. But I like taking the love route because I think a lot of people have faith that God *can* heal them. However, they lack a firm understanding that God loves them enough, despite their sins and shortcomings, *to* heal them.

Many people are caught in the false premise that they are unworthy of being healed. This is a lie from our enemy. I like to remind them of what it cost to be healed - the agony Jesus went through – and how He considered it pure joy to ascend Golgotha (Hebrews 12:2). I'll sometimes even talk about Communion - reminding them that we drink the juice, which represents Christ's blood that was shed so we may be forgiven for our sins, but we also eat the bread that represents the body of Christ which was tortured and beaten so we might be healed. Jesus instituted a dual covenant. This is why, after the friends lowered their paralytic companion through a hole they cut in the roof, Jesus said, "Your sins are forgiven."

The religious people in the room began to complain that Jesus was speaking blasphemy, but Jesus retorted in Luke 5, "Which is easier: to say, 'Your sins are forgiven,' or to say, 'Get up and walk'? But I want you to know that the Son of Man has authority on earth to forgive sins." Jesus then tells the man to get up and walk - and the man is instantly healed!

You'll find forgiveness of sins and healing running side by side throughout the entire bible. One of my favorite passages is Psalm 103:3, which states, "Praise the Lord, my soul! And forget not all His benefits - who forgives your sins and heals all of your diseases." Again, as I mentioned previously, James says we're to pray for the sick and that our prayer offered in faith will heal them, but he continues in chapter 5, verse fifteen, "If they have sinned, they will be forgiven. Therefore confess your sins to each other and pray for each other so that you may be healed."

Remember, Jesus came to "sozo" us - save, heal, deliver, and restore. I don't want to go too deep into this theology, but I want you to be aware there are

more profound implications to God healing some-
one than just a broken body coming back together.
Sometimes it helps to briefly remind a person that
Christ procured their healing at the cross - and
Communion can be that reminder.

I try not to pray too long for someone. I once read
somewhere that if it takes you longer than a minute
to pray for someone to be healed, you're just trying
to talk yourself into it. I can't entirely agree with
this notion. I have had multi-hour-long prayer sessions for people to be healed, and Smith Wigglesworth (a man whom God used to heal a plethora of
people) would tell you that the *gift* of healing must
come with the *fruit* of patience. But as I said, I *try*
not to pray too long for people because our words
don't heal broken bodies - the Holy Spirit does. So
not taking long to pray for healing is more of a
guideline than a rule; remember to follow the Holy
Spirit.

Something you should be aware of, though, is that
we frequently must pray more than once to see
someone fully healed. I don't know if the Spirit is
simply healing the person over time or if God actually wants us to be persistent in our prayers, but

even Jesus prayed twice for a blind man. The first time he received partial vision, and the second time he received full vision (Mark 8). Practically speaking, I love when the person has pain right then and there so we can test for their healing immediately.

I was in church one Sunday when the preacher had people raise their hands for generic prayer requests. I laid my hand on a woman behind me and prayed a generic prayer for her. This did not satisfy me, though, so when the "two minutes" came where we usually "meet and greet" one another, I turned and asked her, "What were we praying for?" She responded that she had terrible sciatica pain from her hip down through one of her legs. She said it started after the birth of one of her children decades ago and would flare up now and then, but in the last year it had become unbearable. I asked her if she minded me praying for her again, and she welcomed the proposition.

I laid my hand on her shoulder and began, "Father, thank you for this woman (I usually call them by their name when I pray, but I'm keeping most of the people anonymous in this book). Thank you that you love her, and she is your daughter. She's in great pain though, so I lift her up to you. I command every bit of pain to leave right now; get out of her! Sciatica, be healed in the name of Jesus!"

We finished praying, and I asked her if she noticed any difference. She was obviously surprised and said she noticed the pain went down some. I asked her, "If your pain was at a level ten before we prayed, what would you say it is now?" She responded it was probably at a level six now.

Our two minutes of meet and greet were up, but as I'm fond of saying, I don't believe in half miracles. I told her I could continue to pray for her if we went to the back of the auditorium, so we weren't a distraction. She was happy to do this. We found a decently quiet corner, and I prayed again, "Father, thank you for partial healing and bringing her pain down from a ten to a six. I don't believe in half miracles, though; we are believing for full healing. All pain in this woman, get out now!" I like to snap my fingers when I say the word "now" - it's a "faith activation point." I'm expecting things to shift at *that* very moment. I asked her again how she felt, and she said the pain was now at a three. We prayed two more times and the pain completely left. The following week I checked in on her and she said the pain never came back, praise God!

I once heard an evangelist named Robby Dawkins remark that if Jesus had to pray for the blind man twice, he had at least seven chances. Christians need to understand that our enemy doesn't roll over and give up easily. Sometimes we must dig in and persistently believe for someone to be healed. This is true for deliverance, also. If you read carefully, Jesus had already told Legion to come out of the possessed man before it started to bargain with Him (Mark 5:8). Demons can be stubborn, so don't give up immediately if they aren't vacating.

A bit of practical advice is to not assume what a person wants prayer for, but to ask them. Their arm might be in a cast, but what they are truly coming to you about might be their suicidal ideation. Communication is key! Ask them how they feel, what they are thinking, what their pain level is at, etc. Ask them to test if they are healed after praying (if possible).

I like to place my hand on people when I pray for them. If their injury is evident, such as a broken wrist, I ask if I can put my hand on the injury itself. Some places aren't appropriate to put your hand, so a shoulder suffices. I've had people be uncomfortable with the thought of me placing my hand even on their shoulder, so I just stretch my arm toward them with palm open. Occasionally, if I'm ministering in a group, I'll ask a female in the group to place her hand on other females we are praying for. In the end, though, you do not have to place your hand on a person to see them healed. Trust in Jesus is everything, and what you do physically is secondary. I've seen people healed while praying over the phone, over video-call, and even over voice-text message. You don't even *have* to pray; you can simply lay your hands on the sick person and *believe*.

As you minister to people and pray for the sick, you'll learn little things here and there similar to what I've mentioned in this chapter. When I first joined our church's ministry team, something they taught us stood out to me. They told us that we should always keep our eyes open when we pray for the sick. The reason you do this is partly for your safety (mentors of mine once dodged a punch while working on their church's prayer team) but mostly so you can be looking for signs of demonic manifestation.

Chapter 9
Dealing with the Demonic

In Luke 13, a woman has been bent over for eighteen years. When she comes to Jesus for healing, He discerns in the Spirit that her ailment does not have a natural cause (such as a person injured from a fall off a ladder), but instead it is caused by a "spirit of infirmity." An evil spirit is causing her to be sick. Jesus drives this demon out, and she is instantly healed.

Smith Wigglesworth, in his book Ever Increasing Faith, tells us that in his experience cancer is almost always caused by an evil spirit. Shawn Hurley of Happy Hands Ministries once told a story about the first time he encountered such an entity. He was called to a hospital in his early years of praying for the sick to pray for a young boy with cancer. As he was praying for this child, a man's voice came out of the boy and told him, "I don't have to leave." This obviously scared the bejeezus out of Shawn, as he had no prior experience with spirits of infirmity.

He did not know what to do, and to his dismay that boy eventually died. Shawn has come a long way since then and is now an absolute menace to Satan's kingdom.

The spiritual can affect the physical. We all know this, but we don't like to talk about it. A spiritually downcast person will not recover from sickness as quickly as someone "in good spirits." The Holy Spirit gave life to Jesus' mortal body and raised Him from the dead - the spiritual affecting the physical.

In the West, we have naturalized everything. The spiritual realm does not come into our minds as a cause for sickness, so we delve deep into psychology and pharmaceuticals to deal with illnesses that other cultures know to be spiritual - and Jesus Himself was quickly able to discern, too.

According to Hopkins Medical, one in four adults in America suffer from a diagnosable mental illness. The two most common problems I have encountered in people have been clinical depression and debilitating anxiety. Our society calls these mental illnesses, and we are increasingly trying to normalize their prevalence. But, in my experience, if a person is having suicidal thoughts or if they experience panic attacks, these mental disorders have always been caused by demons.

A young woman came to one of our Fairendell Freedom Nights and hid on the couch as she watched person after person experience a miraculous healing or deliverance. A point came in the night when an older lady said she believed someone else there needed prayer and began to describe the symptoms this person would be facing. The young woman eventually came forward saying, "It's me, it's me," as she reluctantly walked up for prayer.

This woman had experienced something quite traumatic in her youth which she carried into adulthood. She thought she had dealt with it, but a counseling session brought it all back. As a result, she began to experience horrible anxiety. I had never met anyone who was held so captive by a spirit of worry; she told us that she experienced *hour-long* panic attacks. We began to pray for her, and I rebuked the unclean spirit in her.

The way I usually do this is similar to how I deal with natural sickness - I speak directly to the demon and command it to get out of the person. Pastor Joel once succinctly summed up what a Christian is supposed to do when dealing with a demon - "Drive it out." As you'll read momentarily, sometimes this process takes thirty seconds, and other times it has taken me thirty minutes - but I have heard of sessions that took hours.

The woman began to shake as we prayed for her deliverance, typical for a demon manifesting. Eventually, once we thought the demon had left, we stopped praying. I asked the woman two questions I've come to ask just about everyone I do deliverance on - "How do you feel? What are you thinking?" I want to know how they *feel* because demons do not make people feel good - they are all about fear, panic, anxiety, depression, sickness, destruction, etc. but the Holy Spirit makes people feel warm, peaceful, joyful, calm, and I'd even say - beautiful.

I want to know what they are *thinking* because demons can give us intrusive thoughts. If you've ever known a woman experiencing postpartum depression, she'll tell you she has thoughts she does not want to have but can't help it. These are thoughts of self-harm or harming her child. Earlier in this book, I painted a scene of myself on a film set, sharing my testimony with six other men - one of them asking how I was delivered of depression.

One of the things I told this man, to explain why what he was experiencing was demonic, pertained to his thought life. I told him, "You have thoughts of killing yourself. Where do you think those thoughts come from? Evolution tells us the purpose of a species is to propagate its genes and to survive - thus, suicide does not come from ourselves because we are naturally inclined to live. Furthermore, Jesus tells us He came to give us life and life abundantly - so suicidal thoughts can't possibly be from God. So what option is left to us? Well, in John 10:10, Jesus also tells us that our enemy comes to steal, kill, and destroy." Thus, if the person I just prayed for is still experiencing demonic thoughts, I know I have failed to drive out the demon.

After we stopped praying for the young woman and I asked her how she felt, she told me, "Not well." So I looked up at my pastor, standing in the back, and he said, "Why don't we pray again?"

Again I rebuked the evil spirit holding her captive, and she eventually started to cough lightly. I commanded the spirit, "Go, go, go, go!" and suddenly, the young woman burst out in laughter. The laughter was so vibrant and loud it became contagious. Pretty soon, half the people in that room started laughing - including myself. After the uproar calmed down, the young woman explained, "I've been asking God for months to let me laugh again!" Almost half a year later, this woman has not had a panic attack since that night.

Trauma seems to crack open a door for the demonic to creep into our lives. Unfortunately, western society currently has a massive blind spot regarding this principle. Instead of recognizing the demonic for what it is and *battling*, we often roll over and start to agree with those intrusive thoughts (You're ugly, you're unwanted, they'd be better off without you, this will kill you, life is pointless, you're not actually a woman, you're not actually a man, etc.) Eventually, we find those thoughts turning into actions.

The birth of my first daughter, Ella, was traumatic for my wife. This was back in 2018, before I started walking with the Holy Spirit as I do today. We did not realize at the time that Aly had a narrow pelvic inlet - making it impossible for her to give birth any other way than a c-section. She labored for what seemed like forever, but our baby would not come. Eventually, Aly and Ella became tachycardic, and a uterus infection was detected (possibly from the instrument they broke her water with). My little family was dying in front of me. I wept horribly and texted everyone I knew to please pray.

They rushed her in for an emergency c-section, pumped her full of antibiotics, and began to operate. There was a problem, though. Since she already had an epidural they could not give her a spinal tap. Consequently, she could feel the operation; as she recalls, she remembers feeling them tugging at her organs. My wife then had a panic attack on the operating table, so they eventually put her under. My daughter defecated on her way out of the womb, which got inside my wife's body cavity. Aly remembers coming in and out of consciousness - just enough to hear the doctors discussing how they were taking her organs out to clean them.

Her recovery was not great. A c-section is full-on abdominal surgery. Aly could not go to the bath-

room alone; she could hardly even get out of bed.
Over the next several weeks, she became despondent and failed to bond with our newborn. She did
not tell anyone then, but she began to have intrusive thoughts of self-harm and harming our child.
Thankfully a good friend of ours recognized the
signs, had her admit her intentions to take her life,
and off my family went to the hospital. Aly begged
my mom and I not to take her - like a small child
pleading not to make her go on a roller-coaster, or a
drug addict desperately trying to persuade someone
not to flush their stash down the toilet.

The hospital made her get on antidepressants, and
we also put her in therapy. You have to understand
that despite my previous experience of being delivered from depression when I was ten, I had no idea
this was a spiritual sickness. I bought into the premise that her hormones were just out of whack. Believe me, I think that's a definite cause of women's
postpartum depression - but the moment we cross
from "baby blues" into suicide and murder, I am
convinced we're dealing with the demonic.

She came home, and things did not get better. On
the baby monitor, she would see a demon in our

daughter's bedroom at night. She was even pushed once by an invisible force near our staircase. The doctor upped her dosage of antidepressants, and eventually things came to a head one day when I found her crying on the floor. I told her we should pray about it, and she violently shoved me away, screaming she didn't want to pray. This was *not* the woman I married, friend. My mother-in-law and I took her to the hospital again, and she protested angrily the entire way there.

After evaluation, the hospital staff informed us that she would need to go to a mental institution. They suggested she voluntarily admit herself so she could likewise get out on her own terms. If she did not do that, they would involuntarily admit her for "her safety." Wisely, Aly voluntarily admitted herself to an institution nearby. Her mother and I drove her down there, and they took her back for evaluation. Hours went by. Eventually, I became angry. Why had I not heard anything from the staff about my wife? If I recall correctly, it was past midnight at this point. I decided to confront the staff and they reluctantly let me into the room where my wife was being held. It was like something out of a movie - a sterile white room, nothing you could grab to injure

yourself with, and even the door handles were re-
cessed and rounded. My poor wife sat in a chair
bolted to the floor in the middle of this room. She
looked so defeated.

To this day, my heart breaks when I think about
this scene. I am so thankful to my God that He
spoke to me there - a bit of light in a cloud of darkness. Aly and I were not alone in that room. On the
one hand, there was a demon, and on the other
hand, there was the Holy Spirit, but I didn't know
this at the time. I had an overwhelming feeling that
I needed to get my wife out of that facility. I called
her therapist, who also happened to be a Christian. I
told her I did not feel this was where my wife would
find healing. She prayed for us over the phone and
encouraged me to "seek God's face." We hung up, I
thought for a moment, and I knew I needed to get
Aly out.

I began looking for a way to leave, but all exits were
locked. I knew that had to be a fire-code issue, that
there must be a way for those doors to unlock from
the inside. I thought about how I could set the fire
alarm off and what I'd do if a staff member came in

- would I be willing to engage in violence if it came to it?

I told my wife I did not believe she'd find healing there, so she followed my lead. I told her we might need to lie to get her out - and that's precisely what we did. When the staff finally showed up to evaluate her (bear in mind they kept her waiting in this room for over three hours before doing the initial intake), I told them that she had changed her mind and was feeling much better. My wife wore a happy face and agreed with this; however, they would not let us leave without signing a "safety plan" that outlined what we should do if my wife had mental issues going forward. Done, signed; let's get out of here. I whisked Aly away and told her mother that we were leaving. I explained to my mother-in-law what I knew was true on the way home.

Looking back, I realize the institution was trying to help my wife. But I also realize two more things - first, it is not a place where people get healed. The facility is designed to keep you safe, not to rid you of your ailment. Second, that facility was crawling with the demonic - although they mean well, the people that work there could most likely do nothing about it aside from pumping the patients full of drugs. Without the Holy Spirit intervening in some fashion, that poor staff will forever be fighting an uphill battle.

Ephesians 6:12 tells us, "For our struggle is not against flesh and blood, but against the rulers, against the authorities, against the powers of this dark world and against the spiritual forces of evil in the heavenly realms." There is a demonic hierarchy in the spiritual realm. We know this because Jesus said that when a demon is driven out of someone it wanders through arid places, and decides it should go back to the person it came out of - but this time it brings demons more wicked than itself to try to take back its old home (Matthew 12:43). Did you catch it? Some demons are *more* wicked than others.

Paul speaks about rulers and authorities. He isn't talking about kings and presidents - he's talking about demons that rule over territories. I met an ex-pastor once who told me of a time he visited a Muslim-dominated nation in northern Africa. He was there on a mission trip, but in disguise because preaching the gospel was illegal. He recalled the air felt spiritually thick, and as his group walked the streets a terrible sight caught his eye. On a great mosque were minarets, and on top of these minarets he saw enormous demons. Their wings draped down the sides of the building almost to the ground. I believe these are the authorities, the principalities, that Paul is speaking about.

If you remember, when Satan was in the wilderness tempting Jesus, he offered our Lord "all the kingdoms of the world." How could he suggest such a thing unless it meant he ruled over them? See, Satan is the one who whispered in Herod's ear at night - convincing him to slaughter all of the babies in Bethlehem. He directed Hitler to the Final Solution and put the thought in Stalin's mind that the Kulaks should be liquidated while simultaneously closing almost all churches in the 1930s Soviet Union. It may not be kosher to say, but it was Satan that told governing authorities to close down churches during the pandemic of 2020 and to ban corporate worship of God in California. The vigilance a governing official must have to keep themselves undefiled by the world and on the righteous path must be enormous.

As Christians, we constantly struggle against the powers of darkness in this world. Simultaneously, if we recognize the authority we have in Jesus and are willing to step out of the boat to see a miracle, we can command even the most powerful of demons to leave, and they must flee. Notice how Jesus responds to Satan after being tempted the last time in Matthew 4. He says, "Away from me, Satan! For it is written: 'Worship the Lord your God, and serve him only." The devil then leaves. He had to, he had no other choice in the matter. With a bit of faith, you and I can command even Satan himself to leave our midst, and he must obey.

I knew none of this when my wife was under attack by the demonic. The only thing I had was peace in my heart that she would be free one day. Little did I know, as I left that mental institution, I'd get to see her ransomed the very next night.

Medical professionals told us that Aly and I needed to give our baby to someone else to take care of for a week so Aly could get better rest and some separation. My parents graciously offered to take care of our baby daughter - whom we were allowed to see during the day. So the next day we took Ella over to their house. My wife was plagued by guilt. She kept having thoughts like, "What kind of mother am I that I can't even take care of my own baby?"

She began to cry on the floor of my parent's den. My mother suggested Aly and I go to the hot tub to see if it would help her relax, so we went. It did not help. My wife started sobbing and spouting off all of the lies she had come to believe about herself - how I'd be better off without her, how our baby would be better off without her, how she never wanted to be a mother, etc. Perhaps it was then that the devil overplayed his hand, or maybe the Holy Spirit broke through that nonsense, but something changed in my wife. She stopped spouting all of those lies and said, "Wait a minute, that's not true; I've always wanted to be a mom." She then started to cry out, "Jesus, Jesus, Jesus!" and sobbed horribly.

At that moment the Holy Spirit spoke to me, "Take her inside and have your mother pray for her." I was obedient and had Aly get out of the hot tub and follow me indoors. I asked my mom, "Will you pray for her right now?" My mother has always been a firm believer and faith-filled woman. She would regularly pray in the Spirit. Aly got down on her knees on the floor, drenching the carpet with a mixture of hot tub water and tears. My mother came over to her and began to pray a mighty prayer.

At this time in *all* of our lives, none of us had a grid for fighting the demonic. In fact, if you had asked me then whether a Christian could even have a demon inside of him/her, I would have told you I did not think so. Let me tell you now, I've cast more demons out of believers than non-believers at this point in my life. We could get into the particulars of how this could be and what scripture has to say on the matter, but for now understand that when Peter wrote, "Be sober-minded; be watchful. Your adversary the devil prowls around like a roaring lion, seeking someone to devour," he was writing to a Christian audience (1 Peter 5).

So without knowledge of her authority in Christ, without a belief that this was a *demon* telling my wife to murder our baby and to kill herself, my mom endeavored to pray. In the middle of her prayer, she flipped over into praying in *tongues*.

Now, forget what you've been told about praying in tongues for a moment, and let me show you in scripture why people get so confused about this topic. First, we find at Pentecost that as soon as the Holy Spirit came upon the disciples they began to speak in tongues. The word "tongues" can be substituted for "languages," and it means the same thing. Those around the disciples heard them speaking in their own language. This was a gift from the Holy Spirit so the gospel could be spread between people groups that had a difficult time understanding one another.

I have interpreted tongues one time in my life that I know of. It was while we prayed for the previously mentioned demon-possessed man on my couch. Aly crept up next to me and began to pray in tongues. Then, I suddenly heard her speak in English, "This is the prophecy the Lord has for you..."

I distinctly remember thinking, "Aly, what are you doing? Our pastor is driving this demon out, and you're distracting him by giving a prophetic word for the man." Later I would ask Aly to give me the prophetic word again so I could write it down for our friend. She had no clue what I was talking about. I asked pastor Joel if he remembered what Aly had said, and he couldn't remember Aly saying anything like that - he could only remember that she was praying in tongues.

I am convinced the Holy Spirit allowed me to hear what He was saying through Aly in my own English language at that moment.

You may have already caught one of the church's main communication errors on the topic of tongues. In one instance, I've referred to it as "speaking in tongues," while in another, I've referred to it as "praying in tongues." I believe the Holy Spirit can allow a person to speak another earthly language they do not know in the natural world (or allow others to hear a foreign language in their own tongue). At the same time, the vast majority of literature in the New Testament concerning tongues is around a *prayer* language. So rather than the tongues of men, it would be the tongues of angels that Paul references in 1 Corinthians 13.

The first gift is to share the gospel by breaking down communication barriers. But the second is primarily used to edify (build up) oneself in the Spirit. Concerning this, Paul wrote in 1 Corinthians 14:2, "For one who speaks in a tongue speaks **not to**

men but to God; for **no one understands him**, but he utters **mysteries in the Spirit**." Notice the gift Paul is writing about here must be different from what we see at Pentecost. At Pentecost, they spoke to other men, but in this passage, we are talking to God - and no one understands us (without the Holy Spirit granting interpretation, at least).

This is why many people afraid of this gifting tend to refer to it as "gobblty-gook" or "unintelligible." Yes! That's precisely what scripture describes the gifting as being - no one understands you, and you utter mysteries. I could write a long time about this gift, but the main point I want to get across is this: When you don't know what else to pray when you're in spiritual warfare, allow the Holy Spirit to pray through you. This is exactly what my mom did for my wife.

She began to pray in the Spirit, and suddenly things shifted in the room. Looking back, I believe that demon was driven out by the Spirit through my mother. We instantly knew my wife was free, and we began to praise God! From my wife's perspective, she'd later tell me that while my mom was praying she had a vision of Jesus - her head in His lap. He spoke to her, "I see you, and I'm not going to leave you like this." Later that night, when we got home, I asked my wife, "How do you feel?" To which she responded, "Changed." She never had thoughts of harming herself or our baby again.

One time, a woman came down front at my church to receive prayer. She was crying and looked visually disturbed. She could hardly look into my wife's and my eyes. We asked her what we could pray for, and she told us something shocking. For months she saw a demon wherever she traveled. It would appear in her home mostly, so she tried anointing her house with oil and praying over it, hoping that would be the end of it. But one day, she hopped into her car, and there the demon was again, sitting in the passenger seat.

Fortunately, I had recently heard a podcast where a man brought up a similar instance. In that case, he said the demon was *inside* the person. Armed with that insight, my wife and I began to pray. I commanded the tormenting spirit to leave the woman and never return. After we prayed, she said she felt much lighter, like a burden was lifted. Weeks passed, and I finally caught her in the atrium of our church to follow up. She smiled ear-to-ear, said she had been trying to find me too, and proclaimed that she had not seen the demon again since we prayed!

I don't want you to be ignorant of our enemy's desire to intimidate us into submission to him. He uses fear, temptation, intrusive thoughts - whatever desperate tactic he can muster - to quench your desire to tear down his kingdom. I remember being woken up the night of our third Freedom Night by my eldest daughter. She had a bad dream. As I regained my senses, coming out of sleep, I was overcome by a feeling of dread. The air felt heavy, and I could hardly speak. Eventually I was able to help my daughter back into bed and pray in my living room. I told the evil spirits to go to hell, and the dread lifted. Whether or not Christians have the capacity to actually send demons to the "abyss" or "pit" before their time, I don't quite know. Sometimes I get so angry at them for what they do to people, it becomes what I feel they deserve.

There was a long stretch of time where my youngest daughter, Josephine, would see demons. The first occurrence I wasn't home for, but my wife recalls Josie, then one and a half years old, screaming and crying profusely. Aly came into the room and could not calm our daughter down. Josie just kept screaming, "Monster, monster!" as she pointed to the corner of the room on the ceiling. Eventually my wife was clued in, told the "monster" to leave, and my daughter immediately calmed down - saying the monster went "bye bye."

On some other occasions our family will get sick (I've heard this is an issue for missionary families especially). When we first joined our church, everyone was sick for about three months. I contracted norovirus (my most hated of viruses) twice, back-to-back! I had multiple sinus infections; our whole family caught COVID; my kids had several fevers; we could hardly attend church. It wasn't just my family, either, but our pastors and church leadership team were all sick for almost ninety days. The ridiculousness of it all would be funny if it was in a sitcom.

Don't let the demonic intimidate you, though. That timidity Christians can have towards dealing with demons comes from Satan, not from your Father in heaven. Your Father has given you the Holy Spirit, and He is a Spirit of peace, power, and love.

127

Through Him, and by the authority Jesus has given, you can deal with the demonic.

Chapter 10
Coughing, Shrieking, Shaking

There were several points in my journey of praying for the sick where I became despondent due to my lack of understanding. One of those times was centered around my inability to discern whether someone had a natural sickness or an unclean spirit. I would go into praying for someone thinking I was dealing with a natural ailment when, in reality, I was up against a demonic spirit.

For example, sometimes I'd be praying against a specific pain, and that pain would move. I did this for one woman about seven times – each time the pain would leave one area of her body and show up in another. Other times I might pray against sickness, the symptoms would go away, and then return later – sometimes worse than before I initially prayed. One piece of wisdom I'll share is that if the sickness started around the same time a person endured a traumatic experience, or if the sickness is undiagnosable or keeps evolving, then it is probably demonic. Frustratingly, even when I knew I was driving out a demon - I still fell victim to several of their tricks. As the evangelist Lonnie Frisbee would say – your enemy is cleverer than you are.

One time I was praying for a woman with a fear of public speaking who suffered from panic attacks. This fear started when she was in tenth grade delivering a book report, and it never really went away. She was in church one Sunday and God had given her a revelation to share with her prayer team, but she was physically incapable of communicating it to the small group of about ten people. She cried all day about the experience.

She confided in me about what happened, so I offered to pray for her. The day prior, I heard a story about an evangelist's wife who was dealing with a horrible problem of her own. The evangelist decided to try to deliver his wife, and he began with a very specific prayer, "If there is any evil spirit in her at all, show yourself now." Sure enough, a demon manifested itself and a harrowing ordeal ensued. But, in the end, the woman was freed.

With this knowledge in mind, I decided to attempt

the same prayer. Eventually, I'd come to use this prayer whenever I wanted to be sure a person was fully delivered, and it received the nickname "the scary prayer."

I placed my hand on this woman's forehead and lifted her up to God. Then, I commanded "any evil spirit" in her to "show itself" in Jesus' name. I kept praying along these lines while commanding her tongue never to freeze up again - always to speak the revelation of God. Finally, I commanded her mind to do the same. Sure enough, an evil spirit manifested itself, and the woman began to shake.

As I previously mentioned, shaking is a prevalent manifestation of a demon in someone. Usually their hands will shake, but often there will just be a twitch on some part of their body. I've seen eyes twitching, lips twitching, heads twitching, hands - you name it. This is one reason you need to keep your eyes open while praying, so you can look for such signs.

I have a word of caution, though. This is merely a guideline and not a hard rule. I've prayed for people before and noticed fidgeting here and there that turned out to be a normal movement for them. You can always stop praying and ask them if the movement is a common occurrence or not.

Now that I knew there was a demon in this woman, and it started to show itself, I began to command it to leave. Eventually, I called on the Holy Spirit to fall on her - and she fell backward and began to faint.

At that point, I thought she was delivered of this thing. So I started praying for her body to be strengthened and began to glorify God for delivering her.

I then asked her how she felt. She said her tongue and jaw were numb and didn't feel well. She then told me she felt fearful and panicky.

Do you remember me saying that I've fallen for these things' tricks before? I'm used to seeing people fall out under the weight of the Holy Spirit, and of course a demon would be familiar with that - so it took a dive. It mimicked what I'd expect to see from the Holy Spirit to get me to stop. Fortunately, the follow-up questions clued me to the fact that I had failed to achieve my goal. In the past, I would cease praying and ultimately fail in my mission.

Again I commanded the evil spirit to show itself in this woman. She started to shake, and her eyes narrowed and looked angry - I could see the demon in them. My spirit got equally angry at this thing, and I commanded it to leave in every way I could think. The woman then told me she felt like throwing up, so I ran and got a bowl.

I then told the demon I would send it to the pit of hell, or it could leave, but it could not stay. The woman began to cough and gag.

Coughing and gagging are excellent signs. If you're praying for someone to be delivered and they start coughing or gagging, that is your clue to push in even harder. It is similar to when the person tells you they feel warmth or tingles in their body as the Holy Spirit heals them. These are all good indicators that God is moving.

The woman's hands began to clench, and she started to lose feeling in them. She'd later tell me that when she looked down at her fingers, they were twisting in *impossible* positions. The general shape of her clenched hands was that of a woman holding a book report she was delivering to a class.

She began to scream at me for help - stating she couldn't feel her hands or control them at all. I commanded her hands to be healed. I stole a trick from the night I saw my pastor deliver my friend on our couch months prior. I told the evil spirit to release from this woman's spine. I then reached up to her mouth and used my hand like I was gripping an invisible tail. I stated, "I grab your tail, and I pull you out now!" while yanking hard. This was just another faith activation point - I expected something to happen the moment I pulled. It is weird, but I've heard weirder. The woman then started shrieking.

Friend, this may all sound crazy to you, but things like shaking, coughing, and shrieking are not uncommon during deliverance ministry. In Mark 1:26 and Acts 8:7, we see demons coming out of people with loud shrieks. They do not like being displaced from their home. The Holy Spirit is torture to them. You must imagine they are like parasites clinging as hard as possible to their host victim. Your job is that of a surgeon - you want to evict them, cut them away, and save the patient.

Briefly, I'll give you one more example of this shrieking phenomenon. One time at church, there was a call for those needing prayer to come down to the front. Everyone lined up, and I started going from one person to the next - discerning as quickly as possible what I needed to pray for, praying in faith, and moving on. Unfortunately, the number of people there was too significant for our small prayer team.

I eventually came to a young woman who stood patiently with her head down. I asked her, "What would you like me to pray for?" She meekly responded, "I have a lot of anxiety and depression." I laid my hand on her forehead and briefly thanked God for her. I then cried out, "Spirit of depression, and spirit of anxiety, I command you to leave now in the name of Jesus Christ!"

Immediately the young woman's knees buckled beneath her, and she fell to the ground. She let out a loud shriek and didn't stop for a long while. This, of course, drew a crowd of people. Unfortunately, I did not have enough time to keep ministering to her for long because I needed to pray for others, but many of her friends came to her side and continued praying for her. Later I'd hear from her friends that this woman told them that the moment I commanded the demons to leave, she felt them being ripped out of her and that it actually hurt some.

There isn't coughing, gagging, vomiting, or shrieking for *most* people I pray for, but it is good to know that these can be signs of evil spirits vacating. The *most* common indicator I receive is the person saying they feel "lighter."

Back to the woman with the spirit of fear: later, she would tell me that aside from losing control of her hands, when the demon was coming to the foreground, she felt like she could have suppressed it if she wanted to. But she did not want to - she wanted to get rid of it.

I have found the desire to be free on the part of the bound person is paramount in deliverance. I'm at a point where I won't pray for someone to be delivered if they don't want it themselves. Many people treat their demons like pets instead of pests.

After praying and trying to deliver this woman for a solid twenty minutes I was running out of ideas, so I told her she needed to ask God to take this from her, which she did through tears. I heard her start speaking in tongues at one point, and I honestly do not know if it was her or the demon, but it reminded me that when I don't know what else to do, I need to turn to my prayer language.

I prayed in tongues for a while and then commanded the demon to release her. The feeling started returning to her hands, and the demon finally left. The woman was spent entirely - her body felt like it just ran a marathon, so she decided to lie on the ground. I ran to the kitchen and grabbed anointing oil. I told her the oil symbolized the Holy Spirit and put it on her forehead. Later she said as soon as the oil was placed on her, she felt overwhelming peace from the Holy Spirit.

The week after, God gave this woman another revelation to deliver to her prayer team at church, and she was able to provide it without a problem. Further, she began to sing in her church choir! For several months she had been given prophetic words from various people that she was meant to preach boldly one day. So it makes sense that Satan would try to cut that destiny short by stealing her ability to speak in public. Yet our God redeems.

Chapter 11
Say "Yes"

In December 2019, I was worshiping God at my former church when He gave me both a command and a promise. The command was Isaiah 54:2, "Enlarge the place of your tent, stretch your tent curtains wide, do not hold back; lengthen your cords, strengthen your stakes." In my mind, I knew the Lord was telling me to sell my townhome and build a house. His promise was highly encouraging: "You've been faithful with a little, so I'm about to trust you with a lot."

At this time in my life, God did not speak to me often. But, once every few years, I'd hear His voice in a dream or through scripture - something specific He desired me to do. I knew I had to say "yes" to God, and frankly I was excited about it!

Roughly a year earlier, my wife and I had put our townhome on the market for less than twelve hours before ripping it right back off. This act would lead to one of the few great disagreements Aly and I ever had. I was craving to own land to cultivate, and she wanted a yard for our daughter Ella (almost two years old at this point) to play in. Our townhome had appreciated tens of thousands of dollars since we purchased it roughly two years prior. We found a new home in the small town of Nolensville - replete with excellent schools and safety. It would have been a great improvement for our family's prospects.

Our realtor was just as eager to list our home as we were. After visiting the house in Nolensville a single time, we decided to put in an offer, and by that evening our own house was on the market. It was late at night when dread overtook me. I felt like I had made a severe mistake - as if I had walked out of the will of God. There was no peace in my soul about the decision. I remember sitting in the car with my wife, trying to explain all of this.

You could imagine what things were like from her view. Her husband had betrayed her. I changed my mind about a significant family decision. One moment we were both on the same page and excited, but the next moment I looked duplicitous. We called around to get advice, and the Christian influences in our life told us that if I did not have peace about the decision, we should take our home off the market. In an incredibly selfless act of submission (one she'd later claim she did not regret), my wife agreed to take our home off the market. Our realtor wasn't happy - she'd already received multiple full offers.

Now, months later, God was giving my wife and I the green light to sell our home. But, instead of purchasing one, I was convinced we had to build one. So I stepped out of the boat, said "yes" to God, sold our home, and moved my little family into my parent's house. We expected to live there for a year, but it ended up being two - and we did it through the pandemic while also adding a baby (Josie) to our family. It was a chaotic and trying time.

But God was faithful. We found 5.5 beautiful acres we didn't think we could afford, and bought it. We then started building a home we didn't think we could afford that ended up going $90,000 over budget due to the pandemic. On top of that, our contractor had (thankfully) convinced us to dig out a full basement which added $35,000 to the price tag. You must understand there was no way we should have been able to afford any of this - but God made a way at every turn. We were able to hobble together finishes from thrift stores; we purchased windows from other home builds that had ordered too many, and in the end, Aly and I did a great deal of the construction work ourselves.

When God calls you to do something, your only job is to say "yes" and move forward. It is the best position you can possibly be in. All God is asking from you is the tiniest bit of faith that He'll equip you for the mission. As we built and issues arose, solutions quickly followed. We never had too many resources, but we never had too little, either. My favorite proverb during this time became 30:8-9, "Give me neither poverty nor riches, but give me only my daily bread. Otherwise, I may have too much and disown you and say, 'Who is the Lord?' Or I may become poor and steal, and so dishonor the name of my God."

Despite all this, almost three years passed, and I still hadn't heard from God exactly why I was building this home. I petitioned Him every so often to give me revelation, but a word never came to me. I believed it had to do with advancing God's kingdom in some fashion, so I began to move before God told me to move. I started an outreach group at the house where we'd discuss difficult theological questions such as, "Why does evil exist?" After each of these meetings I'd feel, frankly, awful. It was as if I had stepped out of the will of the Lord again, but I did not understand how. I was doing ministry. I was witnessing to atheists and trying to fortify the faith of Christians.

Do you know what the final straw was for the Lord concerning Israel's first king? Saul was a great man who quickly fell out of favor with God due to his disobedience. One time, right before a battle, he did something you and I must learn from. He was supposed to wait for a priest to arrive in order to make a sacrifice to the Lord before the battle. He became anxious waiting, so he took it upon himself to make the sacrifice instead - something which was unlawful for him to do. He was chastised for his sin.

Later, God commanded Saul to eradicate a warring nation - including their livestock. Saul disobeyed by saving the livestock to be sacrificed to the Lord. This final straw got Saul's kingdom ripped from him and given into king David's hands. Samuel, Israel's great prophet at the time, spoke these words to Saul: "To obey is better than sacrifice (1 Samuel 15:22)."

Like Saul, I had moved without consulting the Lord. Instead, I presumed upon Him what He desired from the house He built. Sometimes even ministry, done the wrong way, is a disadvantage to the Kingdom of God. So I stopped hosting this outreach group after three meetings and waited for the Lord.

On March 6, 2022, I was worshiping God again - this time in a new church. Right at the very end, God gave me a vision and a word. He told me that He would pour out an anointing of the gift of healing upon me that I would not believe (greater than I could conceive). I then saw a vision of people being healed in the living room of the home we had built - Fairendell. It was like a film montage; one after another people were healed from various ailments. I even saw a person stand up out of a wheelchair!

Then the living room was filled with people - too many to hold.

Suddenly the back deck was filled with a crowd of people.

Then our back field began to populate with people; they stretched from the deck to the woodline. It was thousands upon thousands of people being preached to.

I spoke to God, "Thousands upon thousands?" and began to tear up. I felt that this wasn't necessarily a vision of a physical future, but a vision of the number of people that would be touched by a ministry out of Fairendell, the house God had asked me to build. The vision ended.

God finally let me in on the reason He had me build our house. It was far greater than the apologetics group I manufactured myself. People would be miraculously healed! Not in a hundred lifetimes would I have imagined God would bring such glories into my world, into my very home.

Friend, God is looking for someone who will say "yes" to Him. There is nothing special about me. I've made more mistakes than I can count and grieved God in my sin more than I care to think about. Yet, God has a magnificent amount of grace for all of us. Do you remember the Rich Young Ruler in the bible? A young man comes to Jesus and strikes up a dialogue about what he must do to inherit eternal life. Jesus begins to list off commandments found in the Old Testament, and the man has a shocking reply - he's kept them all. Jesus doesn't contradict the man; instead, it is recorded He shows love to the young ruler and says there is one more thing the man should do. Many people like to harp on the fact that Jesus tells the man to sell all of his possessions so he might have treasure in heaven. Yes, that's part of it. But what I've never heard anyone preach on is the fact Jesus told the young ruler, "Follow Me."

These are the exact words Jesus had spoken to His other core disciples. If we care to think about it, the implication is that this man could have been a thirteenth disciple. Unfortunately, he counted the cost of following Jesus and said, "No." Let's decide today never to say "no" to Jesus again. Do you imagine this man would have regretted, for a single moment, the cost of following Jesus had he actually gone through with it? No way! He got scared, though. Perhaps Satan came to steal the word from him, or maybe he did not have a true revelation of Jesus. Whatever it was, we may all agree it was a tragic decision on his part. Don't make the same mistake.

Chapter 12
My House Shall Be Called a House of Prayer

Praying is like wielding a cosmic ray gun. Constantly throughout the bible, we read that *words* have power in them.

"The tongue has the power of life and death, and those who love it will eat its fruit." - Proverbs 18:21

It is by words that God created the heavens and the Earth. When Jesus returns, His words are depicted as a sharp sword used to cut down the nations. When you pray, you are affecting *something* through the power of God. Never, never, never underestimate what your words can do.

A woman once reached out to me because she had been caught in postpartum depression. She would not come in person for prayer or even do a phone call, so I prayed for her on my knees in my room. I asked God to send angels to her to wage war against the demonic power afflicting her, and I asked the Holy Spirit to drive out the spirits of depression and torment. Finally, I asked God to allow her baby to sleep through the night.

The next day I received a message from her that she had slept better than she had in weeks - that she woke up not hating the thought of holding and caring for her newborn and that she even experienced several moments of joy. Her newborn slept better than ever before, too!

That is not a coincidence. Hopefully, I won't cheapen the power of prayer by using this imagery - but in Lord of the Rings, as Arwen is fleeing with a dying Frodo across a river, she begins to speak, and her salvation comes from a rushing flood caused by those words.

Similarly, when you wield them, you have no idea what your words are doing in the spirit realm. This goes both ways. With the same tongue you bless with, you might also curse with. And those curses are real. Any psychologist will tell you that words of affirmation or destruction have a mental and even physical effect on people. What they don't know is this is due to a spiritual influence.

So step out and boldly pray. Stop envisioning this world as a place you meander through until you die. You are caught in a massive battle that has raged on in the heavenly realms since before the dawn of time. Jesus has called you into that fight. He has equipped you as a foot soldier and ambassador from His kingdom to wield a spiritual sword. But, unfortunately, too many of our blades are rusted and wasting away while real casualties mount all around us.

Multiple believers and unbelievers have told me that they feel a certain peace when they enter my home. People who stay in our guest bedroom tell me they sleep better there than on their own bed. Little do they know, my wife and I constantly pray over Fairendell. Our family has seen both angels and demons there - the latter being driven out (being a demon at Fairendell is a perilous job with a high casualty rate.) Aly and I will sometimes throw on soaking music, sit on our living room floor, and do nothing but pray and worship. We constantly invite the Holy Spirit to fill our home.

Several months ago, a man reached out to me over Facebook. He read about all of the miracles we had seen, and he desperately needed one for his wife. So I invited them to church and said we'd pray for her at the end of the service. Sure enough, they came down for prayer. The woman was jaundiced; her liver was in failure. Doctors said she'd need a transplant, and she looked only in her twenties! She had other symptoms too - strange, painful bumps appeared all over her hands, her skin itched constantly, and she was fatigued.

I commanded her liver to be healed, the bumps to go away, the itching to stop, etc., but I felt God wanted to do something in her spiritual life. I cast out the spirits of anxiety and depression - later she'd say she felt lighter. I asked her if she had ever received the Holy Spirit and offered to pray for her to receive Him. She accepted. I laid my hand on her and asked the Father to send the Holy Spirit to her.

Seeing people filled with the Spirit is the biggest high. In my opinion, it is just as good as seeing people's bodies instantly healed.

One time, at a Fairendell Freedom Night, a young

boy came. That night I preached on the need for us
to receive and walk with the Holy Spirit if we were
ever to overcome sin or see miracles in our life. This
child of no more than ten years old came to have us
pray for him. I laid my hand on him and told him,
"Receive the Holy Spirit." The Spirit came upon
this boy in magnificent glory. Like me, so many
years ago, he felt deep peace and love. His head
dropped down. When I asked him if he was ok, if
there was anything else I needed to pray for, he
could hardly respond. Looking back, I feel bad that I
dared to interrupt his experience with our God.

This boy was so radically changed that night that he
began praying for the sick immediately after. Boldness came into his heart! There was one moment
when I was praying for a man, and a wave of what
felt like energy came over me. I felt it travel through
my head, down my arm, and into the man. It almost
made me pass out. I blurted out, "Woah! Did you
feel that?" Other people in the room saw it too. It
wasn't until much later that the young boy who had
just received the Holy Spirit confessed to a friend of
mine, "I put my hand on James while he was praying for that man, and I felt the Holy Spirit come out

of me and into him." That boy's life will be changed forever because he encountered the Holy Spirit. The woman with the failing liver received the Holy Spirit when I prayed, also. I saw a broad smile come over her face, and later her husband reported to me that he saw a dramatic change in her life. No longer was she filled with doubts and depression - she became optimistic that God would heal her. She began to crave reading the bible, communing with the Holy Spirit, and going to church again.

I would pray for that woman at least four more times. Over the course of months, she has been healing. The numbers that track her liver's failure have been cut in half. It is reversing course! Her jaundice is down, the bumps are gone, and the itching has all but gone away. It is that *itching* which I want to write about, though.

The second time we prayed for this woman, she came to my home. I love praying for people in my home. The healing rate is dramatic. I was stoked to attack her sickness again with a home-field advantage. I'm not saying there is anything magical about a specific place, but I do know that all of our gifts are activated out of love and faith. I know what

God said to me - He'd anoint me to heal the sick. I don't have to be in a certain place to do that, but I know that my home is a place of love and faith.

We've built a stronghold there through prayer and petition. Demons inside people are literally scared to enter our door. We once had a man that barely made it on our deck who wanted to come in for a Freedom Night but physically could not. I went out onto the deck with one of the worship leaders to minister to him. He was in the middle of a panic attack crying, "I don't know why I can't come in. I don't understand why I have this debilitating anxiety every time I want to do something good."

The worship leader and I rebuked the spirit of anxiety in him. He physically felt it lift and was immediately able to walk into my home. Later that night, he even had enough courage to lead us in a hymn!

You can see why I like to pray for people's healing at Fairendell. We are constantly praying over it, and we've consecrated it to the Lord. He owns it, and we're just the steward king and queen. So when this woman with the failing liver and unbearably itchy skin came, it wasn't shocking for me to hear her say, "Woah, this is crazy, but when I'm in your home, my skin is not itching." Praise God for His mercies!

Prophetically, upon purchasing the townhome God told us to sell in order to build Fairendell, our realtor gave us a piece of wall art. On it is inscribed the bible verse, "My house shall be called a house of prayer for all peoples (Isaiah 56:7)."

What if the whole body of Christ had this attitude about our homes? When Jesus sent His disciples out, He said they were to proclaim peace to the home that welcomed them (Luke 10:5). I believe all our homes can be bastions of peace, joy, and miracles if we're willing to submit them to the Lord and, through our prayers, usher in God's presence.

Chapter 13
Double Miracles

Never underestimate how witnessing a miracle can lift the faith of another in the room. I do not believe a person has to have any faith to receive healing. I've seen too many unbelievers, or even people from other religions (such as Muslims), be healed by Jesus to subscribe to that belief. With that said, someone's faith *can* heal them. We see this in scripture frequently when Jesus praises, "Your faith has made you well."

One night I attended a men's meeting at my church. We kicked the night off with worship, and at the end, one of my pastors called for those needing healing to come down to the front. I noticed a friend of mine, one I had prayed for several times in the past but who was not healed, come down. I decided in my heart I would see him healed that very night. All the men put their hands on the sick among us, and we began to pray for healing. One after the other, people were either healed or giving up, and everyone filed back to their seats until it was just my friend and I up there. The Holy Spirit was heavy upon him as we prayed. I stopped praying in the natural and began to pray in tongues - aggressively so. Something in me hated his sickness; I could not stand it. Things needed to move on though, so our head pastor asked me to take it to the back. My friend, still under the weight of the Holy Spirit, leaned on my shoulder as we walked out of the auditorium and into the hallway.

Ever since I first met this guy, I noticed he lived with constant back pain. I'd later find out it was caused by an accident. That pain was now starting to give up. I asked him if the pain was completely gone, and he said, "No," so we prayed again. The Holy Spirit came upon him hard, and he felt things shifting in his back. Finally, the pain fled, and he was just left with numbness. In his words, he preferred the numb feeling over the constant pain!

After the men's event ended, I hung around the altar in case anyone else needed prayer. This has since become a habit for me. A man came down to small talk and eventually divulged that he had a bulging disk in his back. I told him God could heal him - and then motioned for my friend whom God healed earlier in the night to come over and tell him what happened to him. Eventually, we prayed for this man together, along with a pastor, and his back likewise healed! God did a double miracle that night.

Another time a women's life group was unable to meet in their usual spot, so they ended up at Fairendell. Once the meeting was over, the leader asked if anyone needed prayer, and I was invited to join. Two women required healing - one had failing kidneys, and the other suffered vertigo and severe ear pain. We prayed for one of these women, and then we all turned to pray for the other (both of these women believed for one another).

A couple of weeks later, I got a report that the woman with vertigo had taken a flight and found she was completely healed from her ailment! There was no more vertigo, and her ear pain left. Then a week after that, I learned that the woman with kidney issues had a doctor's appointment that confirmed she was completely healed. God did another double miracle!

I find these types of miracles beautiful because they show the body of Christ believing for one another.

In the first case, a man who was healed of back pain prayed for another person's back. In the second case, these two women took turns praying for one another. I believe the Church needs to join our faith with one another to believe for bigger and bolder miracles. What would it be like if our churches outstretched hands together every Sunday - in unison, praying for their sick to be healed? I do believe we'd see an explosion of miracles. One person taking a step out of the boat encourages another. What would a church stepping out of the boat together be able to accomplish?

Chapter 14
When Nothing Happens

A woman once reached out to me over social media asking for prayer. She was dealing with several physical and mental issues. I felt sure I'd be able to deliver her, so I invited her to church and said we'd pray for her after service. She came down to the front, and a buddy and I began to pray for her. When I tell you absolutely nothing happened, I mean absolutely *nothing*. The woman's face remained stone cold. It was as if our prayers were bouncing off concrete. Usually, even if someone is not healed or delivered, they'll at least feel the Holy Spirit or feel loved - they are moved in some fashion. Not this time.

We prayed repeatedly, and finally my buddy received a word for her - which she agreed with - but there was no change in her symptoms. So we had to give up and try again another day. After this failed deliverance, I asked my pastor to recall a story he once told me, again. When he was ministering in South Africa, he and a friend were asked to deliver a young girl in her home. They came, they prayed, and absolutely nothing happened. My pastor felt like giving up and going home. Coincidentally his friend turned to ask him, "Do you feel that? Do you feel like giving up? That means it is time to press in." At that moment, the Holy Spirit told my pastor's friend to dip his hand in water and then put his hand on the girl's face. The moment he touched her, she began to manifest a demon like crazy. They were eventually able to deliver her.

After finishing this story, my pastor asked me, "What do you think made the girl pop? It was being obedient to the Holy Spirit." Do you remember me writing that praying for the sick is an art and not a science? That we're reliant on the guidance of the Holy Spirit? This is an excellent example of that. I believe the number two reason a person is not healed when we pray for them is that we ignore the voice of the Holy Spirit. I love praying for the sick in pairs because if I have a blind spot, missing the Holy Spirit, I hope the other person does not. My pastor would have left that girl, but his companion was listening.

At our next Freedom Night, we got to take another

stab at delivering this woman on whom our prayers had previously fallen short. I had my wife with me, and she was discerning well. She began praying for the woman, and the demon started to manifest. I literally saw her young face turn old and wrinkly right in front of me. Her head began to roll from side to side, and her hand started twitching. Unfortunately, others in the room (whether they could see her, I don't know) were not discerning. They began to distract her with one encouragement or another. The manifestations stopped, and we counted this as another failed deliverance.

In Matthew 17, we have an example of a failed deliverance. While Jesus is on the mount of transfiguration, the disciples are praying for people. A man brings his son to them, who has a demon causing him to have seizures. It likewise causes him to hurt himself (similar to the friend I mentioned previously who always hurt himself when he came to my house). The man complains to Jesus that none of the disciples could deliver his son. Jesus then rebukes everyone there, calling them an "unbelieving generation." Jesus then proceeds to effectively deliver the boy.

A lot has been said about this passage. Still, one aspect I've never heard anyone point out is how a modern cessationist would have responded immediately after the disciples failed to deliver the boy. I imagine there would have been many thoughts like, "God must not want this person to be healed." Yet Jesus healed the boy, so it *was* God's will to heal.

Why, then, was the boy not healed by the disciples? Jesus tells them later in the passage, "Because you have so little faith. Truly I tell you, if you have faith as small as a mustard seed, you can say to this mountain, 'Move from here to there,' and it will move. Nothing will be impossible for you." Thus, I believe the *number one* reason a person is not healed is because the one praying lacks faith.

This lines up well with Jesus' initial rebuke calling everyone there an "unbelieving generation." Because of the disciple's lack of faith, they were unable to heal the child. It had nothing to do with God's will. Many Christians like to blame anyone but themselves when someone is not healed. They may blame the person they are praying for - "You must have too much sin in your life, you don't have enough faith (rhetorical question: how much faith do you think Lazarus had to be resurrected?), you must be harboring unforgiveness, etc." They'll be so bold as to blame God - "It must not be God's will to heal this person." But the one example of a failed deliverance we have in scripture ends with Jesus emphatically stating the problem was with the people praying - they were unbelievers.

They most likely were asking God to do something they didn't believe God would do - that double-mindedness James rebukes us for. Jesus is quite clear on the fact that even with a little bit of faith, nothing will be impossible. So the person I blame when nothing happens is *myself.*

Later in the passage, Jesus hints at how we can increase our faith. When the disciples ask why they were unable to heal the boy, Jesus says, "This kind only comes out with prayer and fasting." Prayer and fasting are two Christian disciplines that bolster our faith by simultaneously crucifying our flesh while feasting on spiritual food. I often fast before Freedom Nights because I want to be as close to God as possible before going to battle.

I know my enemy is stubborn, and my flesh is weak,

which can cause my faith to waver. I don't want to be guided by what I see, feel, and hear. I want to be guided by what I believe. So I take Jesus at His word when, in Mark 16, He says, "And these signs will accompany those who believe: In My name they will drive out demons...they will place their hands on sick people, and they will get well."

In fact, when I was first pursuing the gift of healing, I remember being in my bathroom reflecting on this verse, "I believe; how come I don't see anyone healed when I pray for them? Jesus, you said that if I believed, I could lay hands on the sick and see them recover. I believe!"

The real question is, do I honestly always believe? Truthfully, and to my great shame, I don't. I remember one time a woman brought her autistic grandson to me to pray for. She wanted God to deliver this child. I was really shaken by the prospect of praying for her boy. I had seen an autistic child delivered before through the ministry of another, so I knew it was possible (and of course, Jesus said nothing would be impossible if we have faith), but I'm just being honest with you here - my faith was weak. That was unacceptable. I shared in the shame of Jesus' disciples. Jesus would have rebuked me too, and then that grandmother would have brought her grandson straight to Him, and the child would have been delivered.

Sometimes, when someone is desperate for healing and is *not* healed after I pray, I reassure them that "If Jesus were here in the flesh right now, you'd be healed. As it is, I don't have perfect faith like Him, but I'm seeking it."

I must return to my "secret place" and commune with God. I must pray to build my faith to a point where nothing will be impossible for me. Getting alone in the presence of God is such a boost to our faith and overall well-being. As CS Lewis wrote, "God made us: invented us as a man invents an engine. A car is made to run on petrol and would not run properly on anything else. Now God designed the human machine to run on Himself. He is the fuel our spirits were designed to burn or the food our spirits were designed to feed on."

We must have God. We constantly need communication with Him or our faith atrophies. We do not expect to only eat once a week and feel strong that entire time. So why do we fool ourselves into believing we can go to church, spend one hour with God, and have spiritual strength to get us through the rest of the week?

The very moment the word of God hits our ears, Satan has dispatched evil spirits to steal it from us. If he can't get us to sin, all he needs to do is distract us. We'll go from one thing to the next and never give God a thought the entire day. If I have several days like this back-to-back, I find my spirit goes into starvation mode. My faith is weakened, and the worries of this life overtake me. I must constantly seek God, guard my heart, and wage spiritual warfare to maintain my faith.

Believe it or not, it wasn't until I started seeing miracles that I struggled with faith. Until that point, I don't think I ever truly wavered, but at the same time, I never really tried stepping out of the boat. It is easy to say we have great faith; it is another thing to put action where our words are. The test of our faith is not in what we say but in what we *do*. James tells us that "faith, without works, is dead (James 2:26)." Many of us walk around with dead faith because we don't put it into practice.

167

It is one thing to say, "I am healed," and then refuse to take off your cast, or refuse to get out of the wheel-chair. It is another thing to claim you are healed and then walk in that victory. The faith is in the walking, not the claiming. Likewise, when you pray for someone to be healed, it is one thing to finish and leave, but a completely different thing to finish and then ask the person to test if they were truly healed. Asking them to test if their pain is gone is where your faith actually lies. The proof, as they say, is in the pudding. Living faith puts itself on the line.

Fasting, like prayer, is an excellent discipline for increasing our faith. However, I will admit that I struggled immensely when I first started to fast. I did not like the man I became when I denied myself food. I would become short-tempered and grumpy. I would not treat my wife or kids as well as I should have, and I did not feel any closer to God by the time my fast ended.

The problem was, I had a misconception of what fasting entailed. Sure, I denied myself food, but I wasn't filling my spirit with anything good. As Isaiah Saldivar (an American evangelist) says, I was just

"Christian dieting." A brief conversation with pastor Savannah turned things around for me. She told me that when we fast, we deny our bodies food so our flesh can take a backseat to our spirit. But if we don't feast on heavenly food (prayer, scripture, communion, etc.), we will not experience deeper intimacy with our Lord. The point of fasting isn't to *deny* ourselves something but to *fill* ourselves with God. We get our flesh out of the way so God can grow our spirit-man.

After this conversation, I attempted fasting again prior to a Freedom Night. Every day I knelt on my knees and spoke to God like a friend. I cracked open my bible and asked the Holy Spirit to speak to me through God's word. I ate only half a slice of bread per day to take communion. I would sit at my kitchen table by myself and reflect on what Christ did for me on the cross. Then I'd take the bread and juice to remember my Savior.

Pairing the denial of my flesh with feasting on God made sure I didn't become a grumpy man toward my family. Coming down from sugar and caffeine can be difficult for your body and mind the first couple of days, but by day three of fasting, things get easier. The more you push into God during this time, the more your faith grows. After coming off a five-day fast before Freedom Night this time, I saw several amazing miracles. The miracles included a small boy delivered of asthma, the before-mentioned kidney stone miracle, and probably the greatest (personally to me) one of all - I saw my mom's lungs healed.

My mother has had a hard life in the past decade. From being born with an extra bone in her foot re-quiring surgery and leading to a painful blood clot, to central nervous system cancer paralyzing her from the neck down for a time - sickness has con-tinued to try to take her to see Jesus. This latest ill-ness was terminal in her lungs, where scar tissue would develop over time. I had prayed for my mother's healing dozens of times to no avail. But, on this day, after coming off my fast, something happened - her lungs suddenly became very hot, and immediately after, she ceased coughing. She had a chronic cough caused by her illness for five years. The change was shocking for anyone who had been around her during that time.

That evening my sister-in-law came to visit her,

and she mentioned to my mom that she wasn't coughing. My mom told her what had happened, which stirred my sister-in-law's faith. I myself worshiped God that evening exuberantly. Even my dad noticed the change in my mother. This was an undeniable miracle!

And yet, roughly five days later, all of her symptoms returned. To this day, I have not been able to evict our enemy again. I've prayed for my mom to be healed from a couple of other things (terrible sinus issues, digestion issues, and even pain in her chest from coughing), and sure enough, she's had lasting healing. But from the lung illness, I've been unable to permanently deliver her by the Holy Spirit.

What can I say then? Can I blame my mother? As you've read previously, her faith is enormous - she's the one that brought me to Christ to begin with, and likewise, she's the one who unknowingly delivered my wife from postpartum depression. Can I blame my God? No way! If Jesus were here in the flesh and my mom asked Him to heal her, you better believe He would. Jesus never turned anyone

down for healing in the bible. Even the Syrophoeni-
cian woman got what she sought from Him.

The only biblical reason I'm left to account for my
inability to rid my mother of this terrible disease is a
lack of my faith. So I must return to the prayer clos-
et and continue to fast. I must press into my God -
the Source of life - and return with a more perfect
faith. My only solace in this situation is that I know
my God is good, and He has given me great peace
concerning my mother. I do believe she will be
healed permanently one day - even if I'm not the
one praying for her.

I have a final note to add to this chapter on the topic of faith. What exactly do we mean when we say,
"You must have faith?" Quite simply, we must believe Jesus isn't a liar. Jesus told us He would do
what we asked for in His name (John 14:13), and
healing is certainly within that framework. Unfortunately, when I looked at the autistic child the
grandmother brought me, my faith faltered like Peter's did when he focused on the storm.

It wasn't that I didn't believe God could deliver the
boy; I didn't even know if it was appropriate for me

to be praying for the child to begin with. I had never thought about it, and the question overwhelmed me. If I had misgivings, then I placed them upon my Lord likewise. In other words, I doubted. Thus, when I prayed for the boy to be healed, a part of my heart asked, "But will Jesus heal this boy?" and just having that question alone was enough to sink me.

The purpose of getting closer to our heavenly Father through prayer and fasting is to know Him more intimately. My earthly father is a man I trust wholeheartedly. On my first airplane flight, he explained how the plane stayed in the air and told me I did not have anything to be concerned about when I heard strange noises. At the beach, when we stayed in a condo hundreds of feet up, my dad taught me that an elevator is one of the safest inventions we've ever created. When he and I were driving back from West Virginia in a blizzard one time, I trusted that despite the sliding our two-wheel drive truck was doing, my dad would get us home safely. I only trust my earthly father this much because I grew up with him in my life. We have an intimate relationship as a father and son.

That same type of relationship must be cultivated

with our heavenly Father if we're ever going to trust Him to do miracles through us that we otherwise might doubt. We must come to a place where we don't even question whether Jesus was telling the truth when He said we'd do the same things He did and even greater things than that. Our faith must be in *Him* - that His promises are *true*.

Chapter 15
Paul's Thorn

In his book, Ever Increasing Faith, Smith Wigglesworth wrote, "Where people are in sickness you find frequently that they are dense about Scripture. They usually know three scriptures though. They know about Paul's thorn in the flesh, and that Paul told Timothy to take a little wine for his stomach's sake, and that Paul left someone sick somewhere; they forget his name, and don't remember the name of the place, and don't know where the chapter is. Most people think they have a thorn in the flesh."

What exactly is this "thorn" Paul talks about? To properly dissect the text, it is essential that we first read the passage from 2 Corinthians 12:

"I must go on boasting. Although there is nothing to be gained, I will go on to visions and revelations from the Lord. I know a man in Christ who fourteen years ago was caught up to the third heaven. Whether it was in the body or out of the body I do not know—God knows. And I know that this man—

whether in the body or apart from the body I do not know, but God knows— was caught up to paradise and heard inexpressible things, things that no one is permitted to tell. I will boast about a man like that, but I will not boast about myself, except about my weaknesses. Even if I should choose to boast, I would not be a fool, because I would be speaking the truth. But I refrain, so no one will think more of me than is warranted by what I do or say, or because of these surpassingly great revelations. Therefore, in order to keep me from becoming conceited, I was given a thorn in my flesh, a messenger of Satan, to torment me. Three times I pleaded with the Lord to take it away from me. But he said to me, "My grace is sufficient for you, for my power is made perfect in weakness." Therefore I will boast all the more gladly about my weaknesses, so that Christ's power may rest on me. That is why, for Christ's sake, I delight in weaknesses, in insults, in hardships, in persecutions, in difficulties. For when I am weak, then I am strong."

There are a few things to notice:

1. Paul begins by talking about his right to boast. He says he would not be a fool to boast because what

he has to boast about is *true*; specifically, he has received "surpassingly great revelations."

2. In response, Satan (not God) sends a demon (messenger) to torment him. **Side note:** notice we're talking about Paul, a mighty Christian man, who is oppressed by a demon. The modern church has done a great disservice to us all when it has preached that a Christian can't be demonically oppressed. I may write a whole different book on this topic one day.

3. Why is Satan tormenting him? He tells us plainly - to "keep [him] from becoming conceited."

4. We are not told how this demon manifests in Paul's life. It could have been a disease, a pain, mental illness, etc. The word "thorn" here in the Greek refers to a pointy object like a stake or a fish hook. So I would assume this is some medical issue that causes Paul physical pain.

However, there are a couple of prevailing theories. The first comes from a passage in Galatians where Paul seems to indicate he has poor vision:

"As you know, it was because of an illness that I first preached the gospel to you, and even though my illness was a trial to you, you did not treat me with contempt or scorn. Instead, you welcomed me as if I were an angel of God, as if I were Christ Jesus himself. Where, then, is your blessing of me now? I can testify that, if you could have done so, you would have torn out your eyes and given them to me. Have I now become your enemy by telling you the truth?" - Galatians 4:14-16

We do not know if this is the same issue or not - if the demon assaulting Paul is causing him blindness. Furthermore, we don't know if the illness Paul speaks about in Galatians was temporary and unique to a specific circumstance (such as a result of him being beaten, stoned, imprisoned, etc.)

Others believe the "thorn" isn't a physical ailment but rather a demon causing repeated persecution of Paul. On one ground, I can relate to this theory here in that I've had evil spirits harass me unrelentingly in the past. Often it is a spirit of unbelief or a spirit of pride. I'll have to rebuke them over and over and over again. On these occasions, I'd certainly consider those things "thorns in my side."

5. What this demon does isn't as important as the fact that Satan has *afflicted* Paul to humble him on account of his great revelation. I doubt it is a *good* humbling, as Satan isn't going to produce good fruit in Paul. Rather I believe Satan afflicts him out of spite, hatred, jealousy, pride, or some other sinful motive in order to destroy Paul.

6. Paul, a man of faith, prays for God to take this demonic affliction away three times.

7. In response, God tells him, "My grace is sufficient for you, for my power is made perfect in weakness."

Notice three things here. First, Paul prayed until he had heard from the Lord concerning the matter. If the Almighty has specifically told you that He won't take away your pain, then by all means, stop praying against it and align with what He has for you. But if you have not heard that from the Lord, don't consider your affliction similar to Paul's.

Second, God turned what Satan did on its head. Upon hearing from the Lord, Paul realized a great truth - that if he persisted in his weakness, Jesus' power would be made more manifest in his life.

"Therefore I will boast all the more gladly about my weaknesses, so that Christ's power may rest on me," Paul wrote. One thing I find hilarious is that Satan afflicted Paul because of the surpassing revelation he had received, and then God turned around and deepened his revelation *even more.*

Finally, Paul attributed this same revelation to all afflictions in his life - not just sickness. "That is why, for Christ's sake, I delight in weaknesses, in insults, in hardships, in persecutions, in difficulties. For when I am weak, then I am strong," he explains.

Smith Wigglesworth understood how Satan perverted this scripture to hold people in bondage. Here is a story from one of his books concerning this passage and how our enemy deceives using it:

"I visited a woman who had been suffering for many years. She was all twisted up with rheumatism and had been two years in bed. I said to her, "What makes you lie here?" She said, "I've come to the conclusion that I have a thorn in the flesh." I said, "To what wonderful degree of righteousness have you attained that you have to have a thorn in the flesh? Have you had such an abundance of divine revelations that there is danger of your being exalted above measure ?" She said, "I believe it is the Lord who is causing me to suffer." I said, "You believe it is the Lord's will for you to suffer, and you are trying to get out of it as quickly as you can. There are doctor's bottles all over the place. Get out of your hiding place and confess that you are a sinner. If you'll get rid of your self-righteousness, God will do something for you. Drop the idea that you are so holy that God has got to afflict you. Sin is the cause of your sickness and not righteousness. Disease is not caused by righteousness, but by sin."

I'll take flak from Calvinists on this, but I agree with Wigglesworth that our sickness comes from our enemy, not our Lord. Believing it comes from God likewise makes it difficult to believe He desires to heal - how could he contradict Himself like that? There is a meme on the internet, that lays this reasoning bare, of Jesus standing over a surgeon's shoulder saying, "Why are you removing that cancer I put in there?"

In John 10:10, Jesus tells us that Satan comes to kill, steal, and destroy. As I just pointed out, Satan sent a messenger to afflict Paul. Even Job's tribulation is attributed to our enemy. Let's not forget there are teams here. We're on team "life," for Jesus came to bring "life and life abundantly."

Wigglesworth continues, "There is healing through the blood of Christ and deliverance for every captive. God never intended His children to live in misery because of some affliction that comes directly from the devil. A perfect atonement was made at Calvary. I believe that Jesus bore my sins, and I am free from them all. I am justified from all things if I dare believe. He Himself took our infirmities and bare our sicknesses; and if I dare believe, I can be healed."

My bottom line on Paul's thorn is this: Do not attribute sickness, disease, anxiety, depression, etc. to God. Do not say that God has given those things to you. Those are exports from the kingdom of darkness; they come from our foe - Satan.

If God is denying you healing from our enemy's affliction, He'll *tell* you. If you have not heard from God on the matter, do not give yourself over to hopelessness as our enemy would desire you to do. Keep believing.

Chapter 16
The Ant

I own a video production company, so my day job consists primarily of producing, filming, and editing. On a cold winter day in 2022, I was filming in one of my client's studios when we decided to have a short break. On the bottom floor of this facility resides a full kitchen and convenience store where I'll often grab snacks and drinks to power me through long shoot-days. So I collected a plethora of snacks and popped over to the self-checkout machine. Looking down to scan my first item, I noticed a very tiny insect - one of the smaller varieties of black ants.

For some reason, I began to think about how God must perceive this tiny creature. I had a revelation - God knows everything about this ant. I didn't just mean that God knew its many parts, how many legs it had, or any such scientific aspect. I began to acknowledge the simple truth that God knew its thoughts, knew its desires, and even knew who its great-great-great-great-great grandmother was. He knew everything about it because God is *omniscient*.

I then remembered something I read in one of Reinhard Bonnke's books, which I've previously mentioned. He wrote, "We have omnipotence at our fingertips." Dwelling on the truth of this statement and why it must be true (as Jesus said, nothing would be impossible for us with God), a theory came to me. "We have omniscience in our minds," I thought to myself. Suddenly I felt like I understood a gift of the Spirit I, up until that point, had infrequently been blessed to receive. Of course, I'm speaking of the gift of prophecy. For if the Holy Spirit lives inside of us, and by Him we can move mountains through His omnipotence, surely by Him we could *know* anything, too - *through* His omniscience.

The gift of prophecy is something I'm learning to operate in more, so take what I write with a grain of salt, but I wanted to tell you at least what I've learned in the past year since I started walking with the Holy Spirit. First, understand that Paul told us we should greatly desire the gifts of the Spirit, especially prophecy (1 Corinthians 14:1). I know people who are anointed in this area, and my mind is consistently blown by the accuracy of a word they can give people.

Do you remember me telling you about the boy that was delivered from asthma at one of our Freedom Nights? Well, a man who walks heavily in the gift of prophecy spoke a word over the boy's life. He saw a vision of the boy engaging in a sport that took great finesse and explained how God would use him in that world. The boy was relatively young. He wasn't yet participating in any such sport. What shocked everyone there was what his mother said upon hearing this revelation. She told us that when her child was born, someone prophesied the exact same thing over her baby's life.

I've seen people with the gift of prophecy pinpoint exact medical issues in others, so they might receive prayer, without even meeting those people first. A simple word of knowledge can bring another to a place of surrender to Jesus. There's just something about a person hearing a word from the Lord concerning an issue no one could possibly know about that wakes them up to the reality that God does *see* and *love* them.

My wife tends to move in the prophetic far more than myself. So on the night of December 30th, 2021, Aly woke up from a vivid dream. She yelled out, "James! God just gave me a dream!" I told her she needed to write the whole thing down, so I typed it for her as she recalled what she saw, heard, and felt. This dream concerned some of our best friends, who I will call Jack and Jill.

Jack and Jill had gone through a grueling four years of barrenness up until this point. They'd spent thousands of dollars on medical treatments to make them conceive and had even suffered multiple miscarriages. Each year, their friends celebrated new babies while they went without.

In Aly's dream, however, Jill showed my wife a picture of two swings on their new property. Jill asked Aly, "What do you think this means?" The implication being that Jill was pregnant. Aly then had a vision of an ultrasound confirming she was pregnant with twins. Additionally, my wife dreamed a bunch of her friends gathered to pray for Jill – one of them being our friend Gabe who said, "I see a rainbow, and these are your rainbow babies." Aly then had a thought, "This is a promise from the Lord, just like in the times of Noah." Upon recalling this dream, my wife understood our friend Gabe was a stand-in for the angel Gabriel who brought the good news of pregnancy to Zechariah and Mary.

It just so happened that Jack and Jill were coming over that very day, December 31st, to celebrate the New Year (an annual tradition for us). Aly wrestled with the dream all day. On the one hand, she was excited, but on the other hand, she did not know if she should tell Jill about the dream. Thus, she went to several Christian friends to receive advice - each of them telling her not to tell Jill for fear it might only get her hopes up.

On the other hand, I told Aly she must tell our friend. I asked her, "Was this dream from the Lord? Then you can trust it to be true." My wife reluctantly agreed we should read the dream to Jack and Jill. We did so at the New Year's party with several other couples in the room. I honestly don't know how Jack and Jill took it; I've never bothered to ask. At the party, I asked if they'd allow us to lay hands on them to pray for them to conceive. They agreed, and everyone at the party prayed for my friends. Roughly five weeks later (her very next cycle), Jill was pregnant.

During this time, I had seen a friend pray for a woman who suffered from miscarriages. I likewise had listened to a podcast about an ex-warlock and ex-satanist who claimed he used to curse people with miscarriage (one curse of many he employed) - and that demons would go and fulfill those curses. As he put it, he was as dedicated to Satan as we are to Jesus. So I began to perceive that chronic miscarriage might be a demonic issue just as easily as it could be a medical one. Thus, when Jill told us the good news that she was pregnant, I asked again if I could pray for her. This time I asked God to be faithful to the dream He had given my wife, and I cast out a spirit of miscarriage.

Not only was God faithful to bring a baby boy forth for Jack and Jill, but He also gave Jill one of the smoothest pregnancies, deliveries, and postpartum periods I've ever witnessed.

You may be complaining about something at this point. My wife saw our friend was pregnant with twins - why then did she only conceive one child? To this day, I do not have an exact answer to that question, but I have some hypotheses:

1. The dream may not have been from God, and this was just a coincidence.
2. The dream may have been from God, but my wife misinterpreted it.
3. There is still a second baby out there promised to my friends we eagerly await.

I lean toward number two or three. Since this time, my wife has begun to hear even more accurately from God. Just like the gift of healing (or any gift of the Spirit), we must exercise it to grow in it.

The more you practice the gifts of the Spirit, the more you'll walk in them. God wants us to be faithful with a little. If He sees you walking with the Holy Spirit faithfully to do the will of the Father, then He will trust you with more power. This was one of the first things I learned about the gifts of the Spirit - they are like muscles that need exercised. Many want great power now, but we do nothing with the little we've already been given. We're like the servant given one coin in the Parable of the Talents - we hide it in the dirt (Matthew 25).

The man or woman who is faithful to continue stepping out of the boat will be the one that will learn to walk on the water. With healing, this is an easy task - go out and pray for people. Take any chance you get to pray for the sick. With preaching the gospel, many people want to draw crowds of thousands or "go to the nations" but fail to preach even to their own families or "go across the street." When it comes to the gift of tongues, many people want it, but few open their mouths. With that gift you must open your mouth, or you'll never pray in tongues. Then once you start, don't neglect it as I did for years and years; keep praying to God in the Spirit every chance you get, and then move on to ask God for the interpretation of what you pray.

The gift of prophecy may seem quite different to us, though. How can we give someone a word of knowledge (a piece of information we could only know supernaturally) unless the Holy Spirit gives it to us first? This argument has merit, but the day you hear the Holy Spirit tell you something, do not neglect to give it to the one it is meant for, unless wise discernment convinces you otherwise. Additionally, like praying for healing, step out there and pray for people while asking God to provide you with a word for them.

One day my wife and I were praying for a man with what seemed like the world's weight on his heart. God met him there, and it was the first time I received a word of knowledge for someone else. I felt like the Holy Spirit was telling me this man had pain in his shoulders and upper back. I quasi-punked out and said, "Do you have tension somewhere in your body?" Sure enough, the man said "yes" and gestured to his shoulders and upper back. Ugh! I should have just been bold and said precisely what the Holy Spirit told me. We rebuked the pain in his shoulders, and it lifted.

One of my wife's friends once received a word of knowledge while sitting in church. She felt an overwhelming need to go up front and deliver it to the congregation but was embarrassed to do so. After wrestling with the decision for some time, someone else in the audience finally raised their hand to give a word from God. It was the exact same word that my wife's friend had! She decided she'd never fail to act on what the Holy Spirit was telling her to do again.

I've seen God tell people very specific things like, "Two slipped discs in the spine," or "Your mom's left arm is fractured," or "You've recently come back to the faith, and I believe God wants to tell you that He isn't angry with you." Suddenly these people break down crying or are shocked to hear such accurate insight.

On one occasion, my wife and I had set up a phone call with a woman suffering from overwhelming worry and various health issues. We spoke with this lady for about forty minutes, listening to her problems. Everything she said would lead her back to anxiety in one form or another. Suddenly, while she was still speaking, my wife turned to me and whispered, "God just gave me a word for her!"

We waited for a break in her story, then my wife delivered the word, "I believe God just gave me a word for you. It is almost as if you've allowed worry to become an idol in your life. You like it because it gives you a semblance of control and is dependable," she stated. I personally thought this sounded crazy!

The woman on the other end, though, began to express shock. She said she felt tingly all over and that the word correctly described how she lived and her attitude toward anxiety. This was incredibly freeing for her. She felt convicted and repented of idolizing a spirit of worry. We then prayed for her on the phone, and God delivered her of that anxious spirit. After praying, she stated through tears that she could breathe deeply for the first time in months.

I have a habit of saying things that do not even enter my mind, while praying for people. I'm constantly asking the Holy Spirit to possess me, and I believe on these occasions He truly does. You may have experienced this too. One moment you're praying about something generic, and the next you're saying very specific things. You weren't thinking about these things - they somehow bypassed your brain and popped out of your mouth.

God knows exactly what a person needs to hear at precisely the right moment. Most people in this world are looking for *one authentic encounter with God.* They want to know they are seen and loved by their Creator and that there is a way to be reconciled to Him. Prophecy, a gift meant to edify, is one way the Holy Spirit shows them this. It is a gift I am still pursuing, and by the grace of God, I pray He allows me to become a more effective evangelist through it.

You may be like I was not but two years ago. For most of my Christian walk, I believed God handed out spiritual gifts like the Soviet Union handed out jobs. I thought our destiny to walk in any of them was determined at our birth - and the one who prophesied may not be able to work miracles or speak in tongues, etc. This is an incorrect view of how the gifts of the Spirit work. First, they are gifts, so we can't earn them, nor do we deserve them by virtue of living. Second, any Christian can operate in any of the spiritual gifts at any time - as the Holy Spirit deems it. Do not count yourself out or barred from any of them.

We are commanded to earnestly desire these wonderful gifts of the Spirit, which equip us for the work of Jesus' glorious gospel. Don't be shy to ask your heavenly Father for spiritual gifting. I believe He desires to pour His Spirit upon us; it delights Him.

Chapter 17
The American Church

Did you know that America is one of the world's greatest recipients of foreign missionaries right now? Given our history, it is hard to believe, but America is in such a dark state that ministers from Africa and Asia are finding plentiful harvests here. In fact, I currently attend a church plant in Nashville led by pastors from South Africa and Australia. I thank God these men and women ventured great distances to bring the power of God here. Africa, in particular, is an intense spiritual battlefield. Witchcraft, pagan worship, and superstitions plague significant portions of the continent. My pastors cut their teeth on spiritual warfare there, and I believe their testimony is part of why I have felt so empowered to step out of the boat and pray for miracles. Their stories of miraculous healings, deliverances, and conversions, stir my spirit!

America is beyond ripe for the gospel right now. If you don't believe me, look no further than Generation Z. Gen Z is the most "open" generation America has ever seen. They are willing to try anything! On the bad side, this means they are also the first generation to heavily dip into witchcraft (I'd say a quarter of the people I pray for today have engaged in, or know someone who has been involved with, witchcraft). But on the good side, this means Gen Z is open to Jesus like no generation before them.

Statistically, this is a lost generation. They suffer from identity issues in elementary school that I didn't even hear about until I was on my way out of college. The second leading cause of death for Gen Z is suicide. They are burdened with anxiety and depression - and options being pushed on them, such as medication and therapy, are likewise seen as necessary for their *lifetime*. In other words, they are stuck in a horrible spiritual and mental state, while the solutions afforded them only allow them to cope. They aren't even given *hope* of healing.

While at a speaking engagement for college students, I had just finished my speech and decided to hear from the next speaker by standing in the back. He asked the students to raise their hands if they suffered from mental illness or knew someone that did. All 5oo people in the audience put a hand up. It broke my heart. Months later, I was sharing my story with a youth group when I asked the same question. Not only did every hand go up, but the students began to laugh as they looked around at the response. They understood how ridiculous it was for their entire generation to be caught in the same snare. I prayed for, and God freed, a few of them that night.

Friend, our culture is run amok with spirits of depression and anxiety. I think more than anything else; people request I deliver them of these two things. Although the Church is filled with power to free this generation, we have unfortunately chosen to sit back. Many have chosen to even disbelieve God can take something as simple as depression away from someone. I'll never forget a young man visiting my church who stated plainly he suffered from depression, that it was normal for everyone, and that he'd never have it taken from him. He has visited several times since, and I'm just itching for the day he stays late for a miracle.

As you can see, our culture is deceived. Many of us spend hundreds of dollars a month on therapy and pills to cope with emotions out of alignment with the word of God. But God has not given us a spirit of anxiety or depression. He has given us the Holy Spirit, who can not only take these ailments away from us but replace them with peace and joy. If only the Church would activate in our country and stop letting the devil live rent-free. We're not pushing back against him. Remember, hell was created for Satan and his angels - so it is high time the Church starts giving it to them!

The Church must stop ignoring the work of the Holy Spirit. We've invested too much time and energy in coffee bars, free food, and lighting. What if the Church was bolder? What if we didn't advertise our programs and luxury items, and decided to collectively step out of the boat and put up huge signs that read, "Are you sick? God will heal you," or "Are you depressed? God will take it from you," or "Come inside, right at this very moment, and we will show you God!"

The games and food will not work anymore - and frankly, I wonder if they ever did. People can get food anywhere in America. They can find entertainment anywhere in America. Give them something they can't get anywhere else - an authentic encounter with the living God who loves their soul to pieces. Give them hope! Everyone is telling them the world is about to end, that their marriages will fail, that they shouldn't have children, that they'll be addicts for the rest of their lives, and that depression and anxiety can't be removed. Give them the whole gospel instead.

Christ came to sozo us - to save, heal, deliver, and restore. There is more for them than fire insurance that will keep them out of hell. God lives today, He loves them today, and He will meet them today. If only the Church would step out of the boat and tell them.

Chapter 18
Christian Deism

Deism is the belief that God created the universe, then set back and stopped intervening. He kicked it off, but that's it. Many Christians are living today as Deists. Instead of the demarcation line being "the creation of the universe," it is "some obscure time after the apostles" when God stopped performing miracles and intervening in creation. I believe there is good news for us. I believe God is pouring His Holy Spirit out on creation today as He has done since Pentecost. He is wooing people back into an Acts church life. Christians are bored, and they want to know if there is something more to this life than hoping for the next. The past year of my story is a testament that there is indeed something more. And like all testimonies, the point is to tell you that what one has experienced, another can too, right?

My wife and I once prayed for my sister-in-law's healing. She used to play softball as a pitcher, and she pitched with an improper form to the point it destroyed her back. She lived with chronic back pain for at least eight years - frequently enduring terrible muscle spasms. A little less than a year ago, she had heard testimonies of people getting healed after prayer, so she invited us over to pray for her. We went, laid our hands on her, and commanded her back to be healed. Unfortunately, it was not miraculously healed.

But something changed enough to where she had many months of reduced pain. Eventually, it all came back with a vengeance, and one night, the muscle spasms were so bad she had to take a muscle relaxer just to fall asleep. The following day she asked us to come to pray for her again. From the last time I prayed for her until that very point, I had seen most of the miracles described in this book. So when I went in this time, I went with the confidence of the Holy Spirit - that although I still sank frequently when I stepped out of the boat, He had made me walk on water enough that my faith and trust had grown tremendously.

My wife and I showed up, and I asked if we could go into a private room to keep the children outside. My brother, my wife, and I all laid hands on my sister-in-law. I anointed her with a bit of oil and quoted James 5:14-15 to her to let her know the purpose. I then prayed, "Father, thank you so much for my sister-in-law whom you love and call your daughter. Holy Spirit, I pray that you would come now and touch her body. I speak to this back, and I command it to be healed right now! Every bone, every muscle, every ligament, every nerve, come into alignment with the word of God that says 'by Christ's stripes you have been healed.'"

I distinctly remember my brother getting excited at a point in this prayer. As I was praying, he was feeling the spine and muscles beneath her skin shift. It reminded me of Kevin's shoulder I had prayed for so long ago. I knew that experience would forever change my brother because it changed *me* so dramatically. Do you remember the night my family visited the man with the gift of prophecy, and he told me I'd be an evangelist one day? Well, he told my brother that he'd be a prayer warrior. I believe my brother will see far greater miracles than a healed back in his lifetime.

As for my sister-in-law, she felt a warmth go down her entire spine. The prayer lasted no more than sixty seconds, and after it was over, she immediately stood up, bent over, and touched her toes. She began to weep. God had miraculously healed her! There was no pain! Later that day, she'd visit her chiropractor, who would confirm that her spine was properly aligned - making this a medically verified miracle.

A few days after this miracle, a man who happened to go to my brother's church messaged me on social media. He said he had been reading all of the testimonies I was posting and that he'd felt like reaching out to me three different times but couldn't bring himself to do it until that point. He was a Christian believer and wanted to believe God still did miracles, but couldn't. We eventually met up in person, and I went through the scriptures with him - arguing why God still does miracles while revealing the Holy Spirit. He admitted scripture seemed to support the theory but that he just couldn't believe the miracles themselves - people must either be mistaken or lying. Finally, we both had to leave, so I bluntly told him, "The kingdom of God is not about talk but about power. I can tell you about the Holy Spirit all day long, but if you let me pray for you, I can show Him to you." He agreed, and we went off to his car.

I asked him if he wanted to receive the Holy Spirit. He did, so I asked him to hold his hands out as if he were about to receive a gift. I led him through a prayer and then told him to "receive the Holy Spirit." We both departed, but it wouldn't be long until I heard from him again.

That very night I received a text message from him. He was at his weekly bible study, and there was a man there suffering from debilitating anxiety that was keeping him from falling asleep at night - and wrecking his health. My friend, who had just received the Holy Spirit, told me he was selected to pray for the man after his group meeting was over, but he was too timid to try. So I messaged him back with some encouragement. I told him it was an evil spirit and that by the power of the Holy Spirit, who lived in him, he could pray a simple prayer and free his friend of this demon.

The next morning my friend texted me again and told me that he had worked up the courage to pray for the man that night. I asked him how the man felt after being prayed for, and my friend told me he didn't think to ask. That evening I received yet another text message. My friend was excited and said that the man he prayed for had called him to tell him that the previous night was the first night in months he did not wake up in terror. Instead, he woke up with great peace in his soul.

Do you understand the importance of this story? You do not need to walk a long time with the Holy Spirit to start healing and freeing people in the name of Jesus. My friend was filled with the Spirit in the morning and drove an evil spirit out that evening. It changed his and his friend's lives forever because he was willing to step out of the boat. Similarly, do you remember me telling you about the friend of mine whom God used to heal a blind woman? He was baptized in the Spirit on a Friday and healed the woman going blind two days later that Sunday.

Another young man came to a Freedom Night and heard me preach about the Holy Spirit. After, he asked to be baptized in the Spirit, so a few of us laid hands on him to receive. That very week God started giving him visions.

My prayer is that as people experience the Holy Spirit their churches catch fire! Revival is coming to

America. It must start in ourselves, then in our families, then in our churches - and by the grace of God, I believe it will spill over into the secular world. Wouldn't it be magnificent to witness a Great Awakening? To see politicians preaching the gospel, bankers healing the sick, and teachers delivering the oppressed?

Friend, understand that you do not have to go another day living as a Christian Deist. The same Holy Spirit that lives in me, Who accomplished all the glorious miracles you've read about here, lives inside you too. So dare to take Jesus at His word when He tells us He'll do anything we ask in His name! He is our King, and His kingdom is at war with the dark powers of this world. We are His Church, which makes us an extension of His body. He has given us a divine mandate to free the captive, heal the sick, and to proclaim the good news. He has equipped us, by sending the precious Holy Spirit, to achieve this mandate.

The same Spirit that will give life to our mortal bodies at the resurrection lives in us and stands prepared to do miracles in our midst. Don't wait another day. Don't be like me and look back on twenty

years of a Christian walk devoid of the most spectacular Holy Spirit! He is the one that sanctifies us
so we may overcome sin. He is the one that delivers
us from the clutches of our enemy; He is the one
that heals the sick, cleanses the leper, and raises the
dead. Don't go another moment without asking
Him to fill you - and then walk every day clothed in
the power of God. Stand up, and step out of the
boat.

Appendix
Additional Miracle Stories

Dozens of miracles I've seen over the past year did not make it into this book. Instead, I tried to use the miracles I mentioned throughout to their greatest advantage - inspiring your faith or making a case. Sometimes though, I just really enjoy hearing about the miraculous for its own sake. So I've included a few more miracle anecdotes for you to read in this appendix.

The Only One

I was invited by a fellow evangelist and friend named Ricky to share my testimony with students at his Hope Wings event on a local college campus. This was in the early days of his aggressive campus outreach, where the events primarily focused on various giveaways to get people to come - such as free hot wings and prizes. We spent a couple of hours administering challenges and handing out awards to the sixty or more students that showed up at this particular event. I chatted with some stu-

dents one-on-one to better figure out how to minister to them. One girl stood out.

She wore glasses, her hair was dyed green, and her
demeanor was downcast as she sported a brace on
her wrist. She approached me and said she thought
she recognized me. It took us a while, but we eventually discovered we had gone to the same church
years prior! I told her I wanted to pray for her wrist
at the night's end. We chatted a bit more before the
next challenge cut our conversation short.

After the challenges finally ended, I was given five
minutes to tell my story to these students. By this
time, most of them had already left the event, and
very few of those that remained cared to listen. I
briefly told them my testimony - about the man that
prayed for me and delivered me from depression. I
then made a bold statement - that I was there to
pray for them to demonstrate the power of God,
and if they needed freedom or healing, they should
find me at the end of the event.

Another man gave his five-minute speech on the
importance of finding your identity in Christ, and
then the event ended. I waited for a while as almost

everyone filed out of the classroom. Green-haired girl found me, though. As she approached, I asked her, "It isn't just your wrist you want prayer for, is it?" She admitted she had struggled with depression and anxiety for quite some time. My wife was with me and said the three of us should kneel on the ground together to pray for this girl - so we did. I thanked the Lord for her and then began to command the spirits of anxiety and depression to leave her. They did! She instantly felt lighter - like a great burden had been lifted. I then told her I wanted to pray for her wrist to be healed, and sure enough, all of the pain left, and she could take her brace off. Later that night, I captured her testimony on video, where she testified that God had delivered and healed her.

Out of all the students that came that night, she was the only one that stuck around for me to pray for. This story reminds me that God will go to great lengths to reach a single child of His. Jesus loves us all individually, and if that entire event was thrown just so His daughter would come to know this fact, it was worth it.

Man Delivered from Cancer

Cancer is certainly our enemy. As I've mentioned before, many faith-healers such as Smith Wigglesworth are convinced that most cancer cases are caused by demonic spirits. I've only been able to pray for two people with cancer in the past couple years. The first was a woman with breast cancer. I prayed for her to be healed, but she was likewise already going through chemotherapy. Months later she wrote to me that she had an MRI done which revealed both tumors were gone, and that her previously abnormal-looking lymph node was now normal. She said she believed the prayers helped with the cancer disappearing.

Whether or not God healed her through supernatural means, or via natural medical means, I'm just glad she is now cancer free, and I give Him glory for her healing. In addition to the cancer, this woman was dealing with a spirit of anxiety that the Freedom Night team, and myself, drove out of her. I just remember her taking a deep breath and being shocked by it. She later told us that she hadn't been able to breathe deeply in a very long time.

The second case of cancer I got to pray for had a more immediate healing. On my way out of my church one day, pastor Aaron Davis (who wrote a book called Quantum Christianity: Believe Again), pulled me aside. He was with a man that looked like one of those guys you see in war films overcome with shell-shock – violently shaking with dark circles under his eyes, giving away the fact he hadn't been sleeping well. I was asked to pray for this man as I was pulled into an office room with him.

The man began to tell me about his chronic sicknesses; how he'd go from one awful medical issue to the next. Apparently, a while ago, he had come to Aaron for prayer concerning some issue, and God had miraculously healed him. So, when he was now diagnosed with prostate cancer, his wife had convinced him to go back to church to receive prayer again for this new illness. He was angry at God though.

He blamed God for his constant medical issues. I had to tow a fine line between anger toward someone who would blame Perfect Love for his sickness, and compassion for a man in such deep distress he wasn't thinking straight. I reminded him that we have an enemy, and it is *that* enemy which had placed him in such misery. I spoke to him about how God desired to heal him and was on his side. I recognized he was dealing with a spiritual sickness as well as a physical one, so when I started to pray for him I went hard after whatever demon was torturing his mind. That spirit lifted, and you could see it on his face. I then commanded the spirit of cancer to leave him and told his body to be healed. After praying for some time in this fashion, he told me that all the pain had left him.

Months went by and I did not see him until one day I was on my way out of church again, and about five people, including this man, caught me, asking for prayer. He said to me, "You prayed for me before, and God healed me, will you pray for me again?" It took me a moment to remember who he was, and when I finally did, I got very excited, "Are you the one I prayed for with cancer?" He responded in the affirmative and declared that he was cancer free!

The Tiniest Miracle

I have seen people's eyes well up in tears as God

strips them of pain. I've been told about the warm feelings or tingly sensations from those whom the Holy Spirit has healed. Yet, it wasn't until a fateful and otherwise mundane day that I experienced a healing miracle in my own body.

Earlier in the day, I was on the floor playing with my daughters when I decided to stand up and felt a pain in my knee. It was a dull ache from a prior sports injury I experienced while playing a high school soccer game. During the game, I slipped and my lower leg went flat on the ground while my upper leg remained vertical. I was in a brace for a long time; pain in my right knee would come back off and on throughout my life.

Hours went by after getting off the floor, and the dull ache remained. A chore required me to ascend the staircase to our children's bedrooms, so I began to walk up them. I rounded the first flight and started on the second while my knee continued to ache. Finally, in a moment of faith and frustration with my body, I looked at my knee, pointed at it, and said, "In the name of Jesus, be healed."

I felt something ever-so-small shift around one side

of my knee. There was a tingly sensation the size of a penny at that spot. I stopped for a moment to realize what had just happened to me. Then I finished the stairs and began to move my leg around in all sorts of directions. The pain had completely gone away.

This was such a simple miracle. It was just a dull ache - not something debilitating. Yet God healed me. The longer I thought about it, the more meaningful it became. God cured me of something that merely bothered me. He indeed does desire to remove even the tiny infirmities from our lives out of His abundant love.

Two Masses

A very tall and muscular man goes to my church with a heart as large as his stature. At our men's night, he defeated all other competitors in several challenges (such as eating the most raw eggs in a row - he ate a dozen) to win a flame thrower. This guy is a beast!

One Sunday after service though, he seemed to be on the verge of tears. His fiancé was with him, and you could tell she had been crying. I happened to walk past them surrounded by a few friends on my way out, when I noticed the sad dispositions. So I asked what was going on.

It was explained to me that my large friend recently received bad news. Doctors had found two masses, one on each of his lungs, the size of golf balls. They did not know precisely what they were, but there were many theories. The most likely theory proposed was that these masses were fungi. My friend was scheduled for a follow-up scan the next week to discern what the masses truly were, to recommend a course of treatment.

I asked if I could pray for him, and he accepted. The small group laid their hands on him and I began, "God, we lift this man up to you. We don't know what the masses on his lungs are, but you do. I pray, Holy Spirit, that you'd come upon him now. I speak to these masses in each of his lungs and command them to dissolve in Jesus' name. Get out! Lungs, be healed!" I told him I was believing for him, and my wife and I headed home.

A week later, my wife went early to church for Host

Team (a group of people that run the church service by ushering and greeting). I rolled into church
late because I was bringing our daughters and mis-
judged how long it would take to get them ready.
After dropping the girls off at children's church, I
found my wife, who ran up to me in great excitement, "Did you hear about (my large friend)? God
healed him!"

I ran to find my friend standing in the front row,
worshiping God. I told him I had heard the news
and celebrated with him. Later I received the whole
story - about how he went in to receive that follow-
up scan earlier in the week. The doctors could not
find the masses anywhere.

I Need Deliverance

Only two people have ever come to me and verbally
expressed their need to be delivered from demonic
oppression. The first did so in private, but the second went to a Fairendell Freedom Night and mat-
ter-of-fact declared she needed demons driven out
of her. This is the best type of person you could
minister to. I've prayed for several people who knew
they had massive issues that were clearly demonic

but wouldn't admit it. Even when it became apparent, for example they started manifesting when we prayed, these same people didn't want to believe it. Others, like a man my friend once prayed for, *recognized* they had a demon but didn't want to get rid of it. In that case, the man said, "He (referring to the demon) protects me."

The woman on this night wasn't like the others, though. She knew her problem, and she had heard my wife and I pray for people dealing with the same thing; so she came expecting. Many people were grabbing at Jesus as He walked, but it was the woman with the issue of bleeding who was healed (Mark 5). She expected it, and she received it.

The prayer team and I got down on the floor with this woman as she told the crowd what she wanted prayer for. Her worrying had become debilitating. She feared things 24/7. While we prayed for her, another lady there received a word from God and brought it to me, "She needs to renounce coming into partnership with worry." The woman admitted she had come to idolize anxiety itself - that it was dependable in a perverse way, which brought some comfort.

She renounced worshiping this false god, and we drove it out of her. Then, again, we drove a spirit of depression out of her. My father was there that night. Later he would recall how insanely depressed this woman was, but miracles were already underway.

In addition to mental sicknesses, this woman also suffered from a medical condition. She had suffered chronic pain, clear across her abdomen, for almost a year. The pain had become so awful she couldn't even pick up her small children.

After she was delivered from those evil spirits, I prayed for her to be healed and rebuked the pain in her body. Then the Holy Spirit began to speak to me. He desired to fill her. I remember opening my mouth, and words formed which were not my own. I said, "You've tasted darkness, now it is time to taste the light!" I placed my palm on her forehead, and she immediately came under the power of the Spirit. She broke out laughing - much like the woman we had prayed for the prior year who suffered with hour-long panic attacks. The laugh was contagious, and many in the room likewise began to laugh. I took a video of this because it went on for so long. In the video, my friend Joel Cosand asks, "When did you last laugh like this?" The woman, through her laughter, screams out, "I don't know!" and continues to laugh.

At the end of the night, this woman returned to me when we had finished formally praying for people. She said there was still pain in her sides, although less of it than before. She testified that ever since she walked into our home, the hernia had been shrinking. She asked if we could pray again. What faith this woman had! Again, she knew what her problem was and that Jesus could fix it.

We laid our hands on her and anointed her with oil. I commanded her body to be fully restored in the name of Jesus. The Holy Spirit rushed upon her, and she told us that her whole midsection felt tingly. Her eyes were closed, and she was crying and flustered. I asked her what she was thinking, and she divulged, "I'm afraid to touch it. I want to believe it is healed, but I'm afraid to check it." I told her that our faith isn't in receiving the prayer but in testing for the healing. It is one thing to be in a wheelchair and receive prayer; it is another thing to stand up in faith to see yourself walk.

She touched her midsection. The pain was gone, and the hernia had shrunk even more. I followed up with her a week later, and this is what she had to say when I asked about her healing: "I've noticed a huge difference! I've had no pain where it used to be daily. I've actually had full nights of sleep every night as well & have just felt better mentally." When I sent her the video of her laughing after being filled with the Holy Spirit, she wrote back, "I will forever hold on to this moment where the Holy Spirit filled me with pure joy."

The First Public Healing

I've prayed for a plethora of people in public. These are strangers I meet in shopping centers, grocery stores, or parking lots. Usually, their physical ailment will be something one can easily spot, such as a person wearing a cast or walking hunched over. Unfortunately, most of these people are not instantly healed when I pray for them. I don't know why, and I guess I'm at a point where I don't care either - I'm still going to pray for people in public.

I want to tell you about the first instantaneous healing I ever saw in public. My daughter and I were shopping for blinds in a home improvement store when I spotted a woman in a wheelchair working the self-checkout area. She had her head in her phone, making it difficult to start a conversation. When I finished checking out, my little daughter caught this woman's eye. This allowed me to ask her how she was doing. She revealed to me that she had a surgery coming up for her left knee soon. Apparently, both of her knees were completely shot and needed to be replaced from decades of hiking in Alaska, followed by years more working on concrete floors. I asked her, "Has anyone ever prayed for your knees to be healed?"

She fumbled for a response, but the gist was that no one really had before. I asked her if she believed in Jesus, and she responded in the affirmative. I then asked if I could pray for her knees to be healed, and she welcomed the gesture - allowing me to place my hand on her knee. I thanked God for the woman, and further, I thanked Jesus for procuring her healing. I then commanded the knees to be healed in Jesus' name. I told every ligament, bone, muscle, and nerve to align with God's word that "by Christ's stripes, we are healed."

After praying, I asked the woman how she felt, and she said her knees were tingly. I told her to stand up and walk. She got out of her chair and began to take some steps, "Oh my God! Oh my God! The pain is so much less now," she proclaimed. Until this point, she was in constant pain, so I asked her "if [her] pain was at a level ten before, where was it now?" She responded it would be at a five, so I told her to sit back down, and we prayed again. She stood and walked a second time and exclaimed with much shock that the pain was at a level two. I told the woman that God was healing her and reminded her of how much He loved her. I reminded her of the cross and communion - how Jesus died to save us and heal our bodies.

I then asked her to sit down again and told my daughter to stretch her hand toward the woman to pray a third time with me. I rebuked the pain and commanded it to leave; I told God that I did not believe in half miracles and asked for complete restoration of the knees. The woman is crying at this point. Finally, she stands up a third time and walks, proclaiming the pain is completely gone and that she'll be canceling her surgery.

I shared the gospel with her even though she was already a believer. I wanted her to know the full extent of Jesus' love for her. On the way out, I briefly looked up to see a man standing by the exit with a look of terror and confusion on his face. I had forgotten where I was. Most of the people I pray for who are healed are in my living room or at church, but this was a public spectacle. Many people, including unbelievers most likely, had just seen a woman stand up out of a wheelchair and proclaim Jesus healed her. Looking back, I squandered this great opportunity to preach the gospel right there. I remembered how Shane asked God for me to be inconvenienced for the gospel - to preach in public spaces.

Next time will hopefully be different. Next time I will try harder to be aware that Holy Spirit may want to do more than just heal one person in a space like that. We may take a first step onto the water and find God can make us stand, but my prayer is the Church (myself included) will one day learn to take a second and third step - to keep moving forward until we're sprinting to Christ.

Movie Theater Miracles

My wife and I don't get to go to the movies often due to raising small children. One weekend, though, we were fortunate to have my in-laws watch our children, so Aly and I decided to see the Jesus Revolution film.

The theater wasn't very packed; about twenty-five people filled the auditorium. Roughly a third of the way through the movie, a thought entered my mind, "I should stand up once the movie ends and offer prayer to everyone in here." The thought never went away, and when the movie was coming to a close, I became very fearful. I recognized it wasn't from God and rebuked the spirit of fear that would try to dissuade me.

As the credits rolled, I stood up, walked part way down the staircase, and yelled out, "If anyone in this theater needs prayer for anything at all, come to me. Jesus still lives, He still does miracles today! If you need healing in your body or if you suffer with things like depression, anxiety, or panic attacks, I'll be right here to pray for you."

226

Some people actually clapped!

Then a family walked past me, but the oldest woman in the bunch turned back and came to me. She said she suffered with great anxiety concerning several medical problems she had. I asked her for any specifics, and she told me about repeat infections she was prone to having. I then prayed for her, rebuking the anxiety and commanding her body to be healed in the name of Jesus. I then asked the Holy Spirit to come upon her.

After we prayed, she said, "I felt my shoulder pop!" I replied, "Did you have a shoulder issue also?" She confirmed it. Jesus healed her body right there in the theater!

Well, at this point her daughter (middle-aged) had returned and witnessed her mom's healing. She then turned to me and began weeping. She said she was overwhelmed with depression and was experiencing panic attacks. She was visibly shaking. She said she had just finished doing prison ministry, trying to tell prisoners about the joy they could have in Jesus, when she herself was not experiencing that joy. I told her God was going to deliver her. Aly and

I then prayed for her and drove out those spirits. Afterward she thanked God, thanked us, and said she felt great peace.

Persistent Prayer

I arrived at church one Sunday morning, and a lady instantly told me a woman I had prayed for the prior week was trying to find me. I went into the sanctuary and the woman was sitting where I normally sat. She began to tell me what happened to her.

The previous Sunday, after service, she had come up to receive prayer. I had prayed for her at least four times before, one of those times resulted in her shoulder being healed, but there was another issue we never saw resolved.

For the last 3-4 years she had suffered with a large lump in the side of her neck. It made it difficult to swallow and she lived in constant irritation and pain due to it.

She had visited multiple ENTs, but none of them could figure out what exactly was causing the lump. She believed in God to heal her though, so even with the doctors unable to help, and even with her not having been healed the past several times we prayed, she came up once more.

A friend and I laid our hands on her and prayed for her to be healed. We saw no immediate healing, so I told the woman about the ten lepers who weren't immediately healed, but on their way they received healing from Jesus.

The woman finished recalling all of this to me, and then reported that as she walked out of the church that last Sunday, she started swallowing a lot. As she did, the pain left her and eventually the lump left her. She was completely healed! She now marvels in the simple pleasure of eating popcorn – something she could not do before God healed her.

The Most Mind-Blowing Miracle

I've heard of many spectacular miracles in my life. For example, Shawn Hurley once prayed for a man missing half a toe, and then saw the missing half suddenly appear. He said it broke his brain to try to comprehend what had just happened. The most mind-blowing miracle I've personally seen, though, happened one evening when a woman I had previously ministered to, and shared my wife's contact with, texted Aly. She said she had something called Ehlers-Danlos Syndrome. EDS is a genetic connective tissue disorder. When it would flare up in this woman, it would cause extreme pain in her joints as well as dislocations ranging from partial to full (usually her fingers). It also caused her to have rotating hot flashes and chills, as well as blurry vision, vertigo, and heart palpitations.

She texted my wife out of desperation, "I just had the worst flare up I have ever had while out of town with my baby alone. It was horrific and terrifying. I was in extreme amounts of pain...I couldn't really move. I was having subluxation dislocations in my toe and foot bones just walking across the room...my sternum and rib cage were inflamed so it was hard to breathe and caused pain with every breath."

Later in her text she wrote that she knew this wasn't God's plan for her, and that this disease was from her enemy. She said, "I'm not sure if you've ever interceded for someone virtually...but I'm here for it." My wife snuck out of our living room (we were watching TV together when this woman texted her) and sent a voice message. She prayed for the woman and commanded her body to "Come into alignment with the word of God," adding it was being disobedient to God. She said, "I detach you disease, now, from her body, in Jesus' name. We come out of agreement with diagnosis from the doctor and come into agreement with the word of God that says He came to give abundant life."

After listening to this voice-message prayer, the woman texted my wife back, "I just listened. Thank you so much. I'm just sitting here and several joints, which have still been struggling today, started tingling. And I just stood up and a bunch of joints clicked back into place (here she put several crying emojis). My hands have hurt all day and it's all gone. I'm believing this is it. It's gone. I just claim it."

My wife texted back some encouragement and then the woman sent another message, "I am believing it. Every doubt that runs through my mind is just a 'no.' He is my healer. It hurt to breathe, and it's now gone."

My wife texted her again, "I'm literally AMPED right now!!! How incredible is this!!!!"

To which the woman responded, "Girl. This is genetic mutation. It's rewriting genetic code. I am in tears. There is nothing my God can't do. I'm just speaking in faith and won't be taking anymore pain meds tonight. It's over. I'm healed, in Jesus' name."

Friend, if you're like me, you probably had never heard of Ehlers-Danlos Syndrome before. I had to look it up, and one aspect about it I found is that it is supposedly incurable. Yet my God laughs at that prognosis. Psalm 103:3 reminds us that there is no disease He does not heal.

Twenty days after this miracle occurred, the woman reached back out to my wife and wrote, "I wanted to let you know that I woke up a couple days ago and realized...I haven't been in pain. I actually can't remember when it started. Usually stress triggers flares, but despite a LOT of stress in our lives right now...Nothing. Not even my back...which is where my EDS once caused a muscle to rupture...for the first time in probably 6 years...Pain isn't slowing me down."

Hunting the Lost

A friend of mine named Melissa tagged me in a Facebook post. The post contained a video of a self-proclaimed new-age shaman who promised to heal the traumatized for $120. In the video, people laid on yoga mats, blindfolded, screaming, and showing signs of demonic manifestation. Melissa pitched an idea to me - pray for these people as they entered the event.

It was an excellent idea, and I had been waiting for other people to put together evangelistic outings, so I wanted to support her. She, her husband, myself, and my wife hired a babysitter to watch our children, we loaded up in a single SUV, and drove downtown to the event. We had hoped the building was located on a public street, but it ended up being a private hotel. That didn't deter us. We went into the lobby and soon found several people waiting to get into the event. Those few people would eventually become a couple hundred. Unfortunately, there were only four of us (Jesus was correct in saying we need to pray for harvesters).

We were able to minister to about ten individuals before the program started. Every one of them was touched by God, but I want to focus on three stories.

The first was a young woman we prayed for who was there on account of childhood trauma, addiction, and anxiety. We got to know her for 15-20 minutes, which was great! We told her a little of our testimonies, and she was very open to having us pray for her (even though she was Jewish).

I told her about my experience and why I converted to Christianity - about the man who prayed for me and delivered me from depression, how I felt the Holy Spirit for the first time, and how God's love overwhelmed me.

We then began to pray for her - Melissa putting her hand on the woman's shoulder. We drove out the spirit of anxiety and prayed against the addiction and results of the trauma, and asked God to show His love and desire for her. She was overwhelmed with His peace. After praying, she testified that she felt warmth and tingles all over her body - starting with where Melissa's hand was and radiating throughout. She called this "energy," so I explained to her that she was feeling the Holy Spirit - who inhabited Melissa. I told her about how Jesus said He'd give us living water if we put our faith in Him.

She had an incredible encounter with God and thanked us for healing her. Melissa told her it was Jesus who healed her, and the women were able to exchange numbers and set up a coffee date.

The second testimony was of the very last woman in the lobby after all the attendees had left to go to their event. She was sitting in the corner, and I asked her if I could pray for her. Earlier in the day, Aly got a prophetic word, it was just a name, and it happened to be this woman's husband (who came up as we were about to pray, and asked for prayer too).

We began praying for the woman who said she needed deliverance from, and I quote, "everything." The Holy Spirit came upon her, and she started manifesting demons, but every evil spirit was quickly driven out. I then prayed for the Holy Spirit to bring her joy and peace, and a huge smile crept across her face as He poured out His love for her upon her. We then prayed for the man too. He was not a believer, but desired "divine inspiration," so we prayed along those lines.

Both were heavily impacted, and the woman was over the moon in love with what God had just done for her. She was already a believer. They thanked us, and I got to share my testimony with them. Stragglers were coming to the event on our way back to the car. The rest of us passed them up, but Melissa's boldness knew no bounds. She stopped them and asked if they wanted prayer for anything. It was a couple who both admitted they were struggling heavily with depression. We laid hands on them, and Jesus delivered them from spirits of depression. They were also overwhelmed by God's peace, and thanked us.

The four of us were so high on how willing the Holy Spirit was to do miracles that we headed downtown and continued to pray for people on the streets. The most amazing encounter downtown was with a young girl with a torn ACL.

Her six friends egged her on to have us pray for her. I asked the girl if she was in pain at that moment, and "if God healed [her] now, would [she] be able to tell?" She said, "Yes," but you could tell she was surprised by the boldness. Melissa put her hand on the girl's shoulder (after asking), and then I commanded the ACL to be healed in the name of Jesus. Most people, when you pray for them, close their eyes. This girl was probably not a believer and felt awkward - keeping her eyes open. As I prayed for her, her eyes became wider and wider. I then asked her to test it. She laughed, looked at all her friends in amazement, and said, "Low-key, it is actually better!" All the girls cheered. I told her that Jesus loved her, and the group went on its way.

Full Circle

The youth director at my church confided in my wife and I one night about a time he went hard at deliverance for his group. He set the stage with worship and a sermon and, at the end, asked if any students suffered from anxiety. "Every hand in the building went up," he recalled. He then asked if anyone wanted prayer to rid themselves of anxiety, and no one raised their hand.

I teased him a bit and said next time he should start

with depression because people with anxiety don't like to raise their hands and become the center of attention. I encouraged him to keep pursuing the path of deliverance since the group obviously needed Christ to clean house. The youth director scheduled another night to try again and invited Aly and I to join.

A couple of months later, we found ourselves among dozens of 12-17 year olds at their retro-90s-themed youth night. My friend preached a phenomenal sermon about the woman at the well and how an encounter with Christ can dramatically change you. The worship band came up at the end while my friend kept encouraging the teens. Several raised their hands to give their lives to Jesus! Again, he asked if anyone needed prayer for deliverance, and several hands shot up. Yet when it came time for them to come down to receive prayer from my wife and I, they were all hesitant.

I asked if I could say something, and my friend gave me the microphone. I began to tell the teens my testimony - about how decades ago I was in that very building suffering with depression. I told them about the man who put his hand on my forehead and prayed for me - how I met God and how He delivered me from that depression.

I then told the teens that tonight was their night. "Don't miss your chance!" I exclaimed to the room of roughly 40 kids. I stepped off stage, allowing worship to continue, and stood to the side. A girl near me did a double-take glance my way, then worked up the courage to tell me how she was overcome with anxiety. I told her Jesus died so she wouldn't need to suffer the way she had been, and I asked if I could pray for her. I prayed one time, rebuking the spirit afflicting her. She shook and her breathing became labored. After I finished, I asked her how she felt, and she told me she was still anxious. So I prayed again and saw the spirit leave her this time.

She began to cry and rejoice, claiming she felt it leave! I inquired if she had ever asked the Holy Spirit to come upon her, and she had not, but declared she wanted Him. So I led her through a prayer, put my hand on her forehead, and told her to receive the Holy Spirit. A huge smile washed over her face, and God showered her with peace. She asked if she could hug me (something I've grown accustomed to after deliverance), and we hugged. She knelt at the altar the rest of the night, worshiping the Jesus who delivered her from such misery.

My wife and I prayed for roughly 12 students that night (all those who asked us). The majority were delivered of anxiety or depression, and several received the Holy Spirit. A dating couple texted the youth pastor afterward and said each of them was delivered of depression and that they had never felt "more alive."

Later that night, my adrenaline would not let me fall asleep. It wasn't just those teens that felt more alive than ever, but I did too. Satan got slaughtered that evening. The same evil spirits which once held *me* captive were driven out of those teens in droves. They will forever be changed because they had an encounter with the Holy Spirit, just like I was changed decades ago. May they continue tearing the kingdom of darkness down long after I'm dead.

A Prayer For You

In John 21:25, John writes, "Jesus did many other things as well. If every one of them were written down, I suppose that even the whole world would not have room for the books that would be written."

We can't possibly fathom the thousands of miracles Jesus performed during His time on Earth. Often scripture will say something like, "He healed them all." Imagine the size of the crowds, and think about how every sick or afflicted person had an individual story to tell about their encounter with our Lord. Jesus' appendix continues to this day. He still lives, He still does miracles, and He can do one in your life at this very moment. If you are sick or in pain, I want you to place your hand on the body part that's afflicted. If you can't, then just place your hand over your chest, pray, and believe.

"Heavenly Father, thank you for sending your Son to die on a cross in my place so I might be reconciled to you. Jesus is my Lord and my Savior, and I know His deep love for me. I believe He not only died to save me from my sins, but that He was wounded and whipped so my body might be healed. I trust your word that says by His stripes I have been healed. Standing in His authority, I speak to my body and command it to be healed right now, in Jesus' name. Every bit of disfunction, be made right.

241

Every bit of pain, leave now. Get out. Spirit of infirmity causing sickness, I break you in the name of almighty Jesus and command you to leave, right now.

Holy Spirit, I pray you come and fill every place of prior sickness with your power, and every spiritual void with your peace. In Jesus' name, amen."

Suggested Reading
and Viewing

For most of my life, I stuck to only reading the works of dead theologians - C.S. Lewis and G.K. Chesterton being my favorites. This type of Christian reading is phenomenal for the mind but leaves a hole for practical things. For example, I can read about the theology behind the Trinity, but how do I *interact* with God the Father, Jesus, and the Holy Spirit? Below are some books and documentaries I recommend to people who want to learn more about practically walking with the Holy Spirit.

Books:
- Ever Increasing Faith, by Smith Wigglesworth
- Good Morning Holy Spirit, by Benny Hinn
- Life is Short - Leave a Legacy, by Todd White
- Even Greater Faith, by Reinhard Bonnke
- Atomic Power with God Thru Fasting and Prayer, by Franklin Hall

Bible:
- The Gospel of Mark
- The Book of Acts

Documentaries:
- Father of Lights, by Darren Wilson
- Holy Ghost, by Darren Wilson